# THINKING CRITICALLY
# ABOUT RESEARCH ON
# SEX AND GENDER

# THINKING CRITICALLY ABOUT RESEARCH ON SEX AND GENDER

PAULA J. CAPLAN
*University of Toronto*

JEREMY B. CAPLAN

■ HarperCollins*CollegePublishers*

Acquisitions Editor: Catherine Woods
Project Editor: Brigitte Pelner
Text Design: Heather A. Ziegler
Cover Design: LaToya Wigfall
Cover Design Concept: Jeremy B. Caplan
Production Assistant: Hilda Koparanian
Compositor: Express 93
Printer and Binder: R. R. Donnelley & Sons Company
Cover Printer: The Lehigh Press, Inc.

**Thinking Critically About Research on Sex and Gender**

Library of Congress Cataloging-in-Publication Data

Caplan, Paula J.
    Thinking critically about research on sex and gender / Paula J. Caplan, Jeremy B. Caplan
    p. cm
    Includes index
    ISBN 0-06-501621-1
    1. Sexology–Research. 2. Sex differences—Research. 3. Sex differences (Psychology)—Research. I. Caplan, Jeremy B. II. Title
HQ60.C37 1994                                                                93-22718
305.3' 072—dc20                                                              CIP


93 94 95 96 9 8 7 6 5 4 3 2 1

*For Emily, for everything*

# CONTENTS

*... science is the creative product of an engagement between the scientist's psyche and the events to which [the scientist] is attentive ... .*

Henry A. Murray, "The Case of Murr" in *A History of Psychology in Autobiography*, vol. 5, New York: Appleton-Century-Crofts, 1967, pp. 285-310.

# PREFACE

Walk into a classroom filled with seven-year-olds, ask them to think of a claim they have heard made about sex differences, and then ask them how they might try to find out whether or not that claim is true. Then, ask them to think critically about the strengths and weaknesses of their research plan. When we did that, the children reacted enthusiastically, and their comments made it clear that no one had to teach them how to think critically. They only had to be *encouraged* or given permission to do so.

People are naturally able to think critically. How poignant that this is sometimes called "childlike curiosity," as though it were unseemly in adults. How interesting that formal systems of education and social pressures to accept what one is told so often suppress that keen, questioning attitude. The most powerful force in that suppression may be the sentence "That is the correct answer," which encourages us to believe that there is a correct answer for everything and that an answer once considered correct should never be questioned. But if we are honest with ourselves, we realize that what is considered "common knowledge" changes over time, and the fact that some assertion has been accepted as truth does not mean that it is inevitably and forever right. The only way we can make efficient progress is by always questioning the truth of those claims and evaluating both the good and the harm that they might do.

The exercise with seven-year-olds was done because, years ago, when Jeremy was in second grade, he heard Paula talking about her research in psychology and asked why they didn't learn that kind of science in school. He asked Paula to visit his class and discuss some of that work with them. She had been teaching the fundamentals of critical thinking about research on sex and gender to undergraduates since 1980 and later to graduate students. When Paula approached his teacher about Jeremy's suggestion, the teacher naively replied, "Well, you can try, but kids this age can't think abstractly." When Paula asked the students to think of claims they had heard about sex differences, one they mentioned was, "Boys are ruder than girls." Paula then said, "Today, we are going to do what scientists do. We are going to try to find out whether or not that is true." She asked them how they might explore the topic of sex differences in rudeness, and they decided, "We could go to a house where there is a brother and a sister, and while they are eating dinner, we could make a mark every time the boy is rude and every time the girl is rude." Paula then said, "Let's suppose we did that and found that the boy was rude 8 times, and the girl was rude 5 times. Would we have proven that boys are ruder than girls?"

Many of the children began to say "yes" but then stopped, looked quizzical, and said, "Not really." All Paula had to do was ask, "Why not?" and "Anything else?" repeatedly, and the children came up with a remarkably sophisticated critique of their research proposal. They pointed out that it might be that only in that particular family or only at dinner was the boy the ruder of the two children. They wondered whether one child or both might be behaving differently because there was someone else there taking notes about their actions. They even debated whether or not 8 was "all that much" bigger than 5, getting into statistical questions in that way.

As a result of the students' eagerness and performance, Paula worked with Margaret Secord on writing up the directions for this exercise in the form of a curriculum unit for grade-school children (Caplan, P. J.; Secord-Gilbert, M., Staton, P. [1990]. *Teaching children to think critically about sexism and other forms of bias.* Toronto: Green Dragon Press) and then testing its effectiveness with many other children and teachers. When Secord (Secord, M. J. [1987]. Teaching children critical thinking. Unpublished master's thesis, Ontario Institute for Studies in Education, University of Toronto) asked grade-school teachers to do the exercise in a single class period, she found that the children who had been exposed to that exercise were more likely than other children to think critically about claims made about other group differences (ageist, racist, etc.) as well as sexist ones.

We both have always felt a sense of excitement and discovery when engaging in critical thinking about research and about theories. Those people who have been most instrumental in encouraging such thinking in us have enriched our lives immeasurably: for Paula—my parents, Tac and Jerry Caplan; my uncle, Bill Karchmer; and my teachers, Jack Bush, Donal Stanton, and Bruce Baker; and for Jeremy—my great-uncle, Bill Karchmer, and many others. We offer this book in the hope that it will do the same for you.

## Acknowledgments

The authors wish to thank Jennifer Chambers for her assistance with portions of the manuscript; Emily Julia Caplan, and June Larkin for their thoughtful comments and suggestions throughout the entire manuscript; Gina Feldberg for help with some concepts and references; and our editor Catherine Woods for her help and support. Thanks also to the following reviewers for their suggestions: Claire Etaugh, Bradley University; Terri D. Fisher, Ph.D., Ohio State University at Mansfield; Karen G. Howe, Trenton State College; Lois Muir, University of Wisconsin; Rose Preciado, Mt. San Antonio College; and Cecelia K. Yoder, Ph.D., Oklahoma City Community College.

*Paula J. Caplan*
*Jeremy B. Caplan*

# THINKING CRITICALLY ABOUT RESEARCH ON SEX AND GENDER

# CHAPTER ONE

# INTRODUCTION

## ❖ THE CYCLE OF BIAS

It is virtually impossible to grow up without believing that girls and boys, men and women, differ—not only physically but also in important aspects of behavior, attitudes, and abilities. Whether or not we realize it, many of these beliefs come to us directly or indirectly from scientific research on sex and gender. Because the most prevalent twentieth-century attitude toward scientists is that they discover and describe the Truth, it may not occur to us to question what we think are scientific truths. This unquestioning acceptance of scientists' pronouncements about sex and gender differences affects every aspect of our private and public lives, since—consciously or unconsciously— every time we interact with another person, we are making assumptions about what is true and natural for people depending on their sex. Countless people of both sexes invest great amounts of energy worrying about whether they themselves are doing, feeling, and believing what members of their sex are "supposed" to do, are naturally meant to do, are destined by their genes and hormones to do. When we believe that these sex-related patterns have been proven by researchers to be pervasive and inevitable, it can be disturbing to find that we, or people with whom we live or work, do not fit the patterns.

However, scientists do not simply discover and describe the Truth. Like everyone else, scientists who study sex and gender grew up learning what women and men are "supposed" to be like. They might have heard, for example, that boys don't want to play with dolls (unless the dolls have guns), and that girls cannot play hockey. These beliefs about how people are or should be influence how scientists do their research, how they see and describe the world. A girl and a boy could be doing exactly the same thing, but because one is a girl and one is a boy the activity may be described differently. For example, a girl playing with fire may be said to be demonstrating her inborn desire to cook, while if a boy plays with fire he would probably be called a natural fireman or naturally daring. It is often mistakenly assumed that scientists are able to be free from such bias—to be "objective" and able to see the world without being influenced by their own thoughts or feelings about it. Yet many psychologists do things such as appreciatively labeling as *assertiveness* such behavior in men as interrupting other people, which others might call *rudeness.* Whichever label one chooses in such a case reflects one's experiences and perspective. The truth is that no one is free from bias, but scientists often present their interpretations of their research as though they are absolutely and objectively true. Then, people hear researchers' claims about sex differences, assume they are true, and raise their children accordingly; and some of those children become scientists who investigate sex differences, and thus the cycle of bias continues.

This book is about how scientists have looked at women and men. Scientific research is intended to be a way of trying to find out the truth about the world. It is a way of asking questions and seeking answers. The thoughts and feelings of scientists influence what questions they ask and how they are answered. For instance, the research question, "Do women's cognitive abilities decline when they are premenstrual?" is likely to yield answers that may cast women in a bad light. By contrast, the question, "Do females' and males' cognitive abilities show cyclical patterns over time?" may yield information from which one might draw rather different conclusions. The answers we get always depend partly on the way we ask the questions.

In the midst of the twentieth century's information explosion, it has become impossible for any one person to stay informed of the results and the strengths and weaknesses of all the research that is important in our lives. Therefore, we often accept some scientists' claims as facts, not knowing that their approaches were narrow, biased, or otherwise limited. That means that our view of reality has become distorted. The purpose of this book is to assist those who wish to expand their vision by questioning some of the "facts" most of us have heard about males and females. Practicing a questioning, thoughtful approach to issues of sex and gender, and learning some of the common pitfalls in that area, is also helpful in developing the capacity to do careful thinking about other issues that are replete with bias, such as the work on race, class, age, sexual orientation, and so on. The critical thinking skills presented in this book can help us not just in knowing what to ask about research reports in scholarly journals but also in thinking about claims that are made in the popular media, by our co-workers, and by our friends and family and that can affect our feelings, our personal lives, and our experiences at school and work.

## ❖ TWO DANGEROUS ASSUMPTIONS

As you read and think about the research on sex differences, you will need to be aware of two major but *wrong* assumptions that have muddied our understanding of this work. They are:

**1.** The assumption that if we find a "sex difference" in some ability or kind of behavior, that means that all males do a particular thing and all females do some quite different thing (e.g., all males are aggressive, and all females are passive and peace-loving). If asked directly, most researchers would probably acknowledge that in every realm of psychological research, females' and males' test scores or behavior overlap a great deal. Finding a "sex difference" does not mean finding that all women are one way and all men are another way (Hochschild, 1973). For instance, even when a research team reports that men are more aggressive than women, that does *not* mean that *no* women are aggressive and *all* men are aggressive, nor does it mean that all men are aggressive to the same degree. But we need to remind ourselves repeatedly that few researchers or laypeople remember how much of males' and females' behavior is similar—or, in other words, how much overlap there is—when we hear the term *sex differences.* Hearing about a study that "proves" there is a sex difference in math ability, for instance, we often come to expect most or all females to perform worse than most or all males on math tests, although in fact the overlap in their scores is extensive. What is commonly called a *sex difference* is the difference between the *average* score of the women who were studied and the *average* score of the men who were studied. An average score is reached by adding up all the individual scores and dividing by the number of individuals. Most individual women and men do not have scores (or behavior) exactly like the average score for their sex. This means that even when a "sex difference" is found in a study, we can't predict how any individual will behave if all we know is the person's sex.

Another reason that most sex differences seem more extreme and dramatic than they really are is a result of the way most research is done. Researchers are more likely to predict that they will find *differences* than *similarities* between groups. They tend to look for differences because, if we give boys and girls a test and find that the sexes perform differently on it, we will probably get little argument if we claim to have found a sex difference. But if we give them a test and find that they do *not* perform differently, then it is harder to claim that there is no sex difference in the ability or behavior that that test is supposed to measure. It is very hard to prove convincingly that a difference between any two groups does *not* exist, since it is possible that there is a difference but you missed it. People can always make such claims as, "You didn't test *enough* children to get a difference; there probably is a sex difference, but it is small" or "Maybe that just wasn't a very good test for measuring skill or behavior X" or "Maybe the children you tested are not typical of most children." The term that is used to refer to trying to prove that there is *no* difference is *trying to prove the null hypothesis.*

**2.** The assumption that sex differences are biologically based and, therefore, inevitable and unchangeable. This is an unfounded assumption. Many differences result from the different ways girls and boys are raised, and even differences that *may* have *some* biological basis—such as differences in height—have been shown to be fairly easy to modify (Hubbard, 1990; Hubbard et al., 1982). In fact, although we tend to think that nothing changes our genes, biologists now know that genes can be changed by the chemical processes in genes near to them. This means that what seems to be a simple, straightforward question—"Is a particular sex difference caused by biology or by the environment?"—is not really so simple. As biologist Margaret Thompson has said, "The environment of genes is other genes."

It is important to understand that it is not so easy to distinguish the contributions of nature or genes from those of socialization, experience, or other environmental factors, because some people are quick to claim that what is biologically caused is not only natural and inevitable but even morally right.

For instance, some people have claimed that it is *natural* for women to stay at home fulltime to raise children while men leave home all day to work for pay. Some people believe that what leads to this sex difference (which isn't even very common these days) is the fact that women carry the fetus and then nurse the newborn. These same people believe that pregnant women and nursing mothers have no business being in the workplace; they tend to think that we would be tampering with Mother Nature if we tried to change that pattern, and even that that would be morally wrong. In contrast, others believe that the woman-at-home and man-in-the-workplace division came about because employers have historically paid men higher salaries than women, and so families with young children have found that it makes sense economically for the man to do the paid work; the people who believe that do not tend to feel so uncomfortable about deviations from that pattern, they don't tend to think that a deviation is morally wrong or unnatural, and they sometimes even think that what is morally wrong is paying men more than women for doing the same kind of work.

## ❖ WHAT YOU WILL LEARN

In this section we explain the details of the main goal of this book: to teach you to think critically about sex and gender. Subsequent chapters are directed at different aspects of achieving this goal. The chapters constitute a cumulative learning experience, but each stands on its own as well. To be able to deal adequately with the science of men and women, it is important to be aware of the variety of factors that are involved in the scientific process. In this way, you will learn the essential skills for making critical judgments of your own.

What do we mean by *sex* and *gender*? We shall use *sex* to refer to the biological sex of the individual—whether a person is born physically female or male. Sex is determined by the genes. In most, but not all, cultures, people assume that there are only two sexes: male and female. (In North America, most people think that females have two X chromosomes and males have one X and one Y chromosome, although in fact more than two genetic sex types do occur more often than most laypeople realize.) We shall use *gender* to refer to the social role of being a woman or being a man. Gender means "being feminine" or "being masculine," standards that look different in different societies. Gender is composed of the whole list of features that the society in question labels as appropriate for, or typical of, one sex (but not the other, or more than the other), including feelings, attitudes, behavior, interests, clothing, and so on. The issue of how biological sex and social gender interact—how much our "masculine" or "feminine" behavior is unavoidably determined by our physical sex—underlies most of the controversies in the science of sex and gender.

In this book, as you learn to think critically about the scientific study of sex and gender, our specific goals are for you to:

1. learn how science is conducted—both actually and ideally;

2. become increasingly able to evaluate scientists' work (for example, to recognize that no scientist—and, therefore, no science—is completely free of prior expectations);

3. develop the conceptual tools you need in order to think critically about research;

4. question people's (especially scientists') expectations of and perspectives on women and men;

5. develop an awareness of the limitations of any individual perspective and use this awareness to analyze the limitations in perspective of all sources of information: TV, newspapers, scientific journals, and other types of media. This means ascertaining and questioning every author's frame of reference;

6. come to treat your own and others' expectations of men and women as theories, not facts, which may be confirmed or challenged by the use of logic and evidence;

7. become able to evaluate these hypotheses, or working assumptions, for their usefulness in discovering some aspect of truth;

8. learn to discuss all the different ways any given hypothesis could be tested;

9. increase your awareness of the scope or limitations of the methods used to test any particular theory (i.e., If a different test had been used, how might the results have been different?);

10. want to strive to generate as many different interpretations of the evidence as possible;

11. apply your critical analysis to statements made by scientists, or by people in everyday life, about the nature of women and men;

12. examine how language influences our perceptions of men and women, as well as how our perceptions of women and men influence our use of language about them;

13. explore the impact our beliefs about women and men have had on scientific theory and practice; and

**14.** consider how scientific theories of sex and gender have affected, and continue to affect, our lives.

Everyone who develops the ability to do these kinds of thinking—be they researchers or laypeople who hear the claims of researchers—acquires the power to help stop the cycle of bias.

## ❖ OUTLINE OF THE TEXT

*Thinking Critically About Research on Sex and Gender* begins with a summary of this book and what you can expect to learn as you use it.

The second chapter is a history of the science of sex differences. Understanding the science of the nineteenth century helps us to see clearly that science can be used to prove a point that has profound social and political consequences. For instance, when we read about scientists' intensive efforts in the nineteenth century to prove that men's brains were bigger than women's—and that, therefore, men were smarter than women—we may think it is a quaint example of unsophisticated research from the olden days; but once we are familiar with that research effort, we can more easily see the bias and the political or social consequences of research in our own era on sex differences in the size of *one particular segment of one part* of the brain. We now recognize that the nineteenth-century science that was used to "prove" that men were smarter than women was filled with or based on faulty logic and primitive research methods. Analyzing the biased science of the nineteenth century sharpens our ability to question modern science. Learning about this history also reveals the roots of today's scientists' attitudes toward women and men.

The third chapter is a description of *scientific method*—the way of doing scientific research—and some of the most common mistakes scientists make in their research on sex and gender.

The rest of the book deals with some of the most important current issues in the science of sex and gender. Some chapters are about sex differences; others are about women. Some include a focus on men, but the reason that we focus here somewhat more on females than on males is that the focus of most research has actually been on males. The major exception to the male-oriented focus of traditional researchers has been research that has been focused on women's and girls' supposed inferiority or pathology. In some chapters, we choose a single piece of research and examine it in great detail. In those chapters, the studies were chosen because they have been extremely influential, because they illustrate many of the research errors made in the field, or both. The topics covered in the following chapters include:

*Math ability.* Males are generally said to be superior to females in math ability. Some scientists say this is determined by a variety of social influences, including how girls *and* boys are encouraged in their math studies, whether they are taught math by teachers of their own sex, and whether being good at math is valued equally for boys and for girls. Other scientists consider biology to be the major factor determining males' superiority to females on some tests of mathematical ability.

*Spatial ability.* The ability to read maps or find one's way through mazes and other similar abilities are said by some to be another arena of males' innate superiority. Other researchers say that spatial abilities have been tested in ways that favor males and that when other tests are used the results are different. From this point of view, sex differences that are found in spatial abilities can be explained by the different experiences of girls and boys.

*Women and masochism.* Some scientists have suggested that women enjoy being hurt. This theory has been challenged by those who say that women stay in harmful or upsetting situations for various reasons, not one of which is enjoyment of misery.

*Males and aggression.* Many researchers conclude that males are "naturally" more aggressive than females, but the research results vary with aggression.

*Mother-blame.* The majority of explanations for the emotional problems of both adults and young people are based on mother-blame. Why *is* that, and what other factors could be involved?

*Women and hormones.* Many people, including many scientists, believe that women are mentally and emotionally unbalanced because of their menstrual cycle. Some researchers challenge this idea, suggesting that social influences, not hormones, cause the symptoms, also noting that men's hormonal cycles do not get the same attention as do women's.

*Verbal ability.* One of the few realms in which females have been considered superior is that of verbal ability. But even that supposed *advantage* has been used against women, and the research is riddled with problems.

*Dependence of females.* Girls and women have long been regarded as the more dependent sex, but recent work suggests that much of the relevant research actually shows them to be *skilled in forming and maintaining relationships* rather than dependent.

## ❖ KEEPING SEX DIFFERENCES IN PERSPECTIVE

When we study the research on sex differences, we can get so absorbed in thinking about the details of the studies that we lose sight of the larger perspective. Part of the larger perspective that we need to keep in mind is that, since each scientist will be able to explore only a limited number of research questions, there must be a reason that some choose to spend their lives trying to find sex and gender differences.

Since most "proof" of differences between groups is usually used to "prove" that one group is *better than* the other, and scientists are aware of this, we need to ask what motivates them to pursue such research. A few hope to prove that there are fewer sex differences than people thought there were; many, however, seem to be intent on justifying the treatment of females as inferior in terms of being, for instance, less intelligent, "overly emotional," or more dependent than males. Scientists who try to prove that there are important differences between members of different *races* are usually recognized, these days, as racist, but those who try to prove that there are important sex differences are not usually recognized as sexist.

Another part of the perspective that we need to maintain involves a clear view of *which* research questions become the focus of the greatest amount of research. For example, although early sex-difference researchers reported that females were superior to males in various verbal abilities (e.g., learning to speak at younger ages, developing greater vocabularies) and that males were superior to females in spatial abilities, *most* of the research effort has gone into work on spatial abilities. So has most of the attention from the media. The research effort has included trying to document how great the male superiority is and developing theories to explain why males are so superior in this regard. If we become caught up in exploring the details of the spatial abilities research, we fall into the trap of *assuming* that males are superior, forgetting that there is also evidence that females are superior to males. The goal should not be to reverse the pattern and focus on areas where females outperform males; rather, it should be to take care not to let our beliefs be shaped by the research topics that receive the most attention from scientists and from the media reports about them.

We do not claim that there are definitely no sex differences in humans' behavior. What we do believe is that, since so much of the research is deeply flawed, and since males and females have nowhere been treated identically from birth, it is virtually impossible to know what inevitable sex differences there might be. And if it seems to you, as you read this book, that most sex-difference research is riddled with problems, you are right. This is partly because of the difficulty of studying human behavior, which is so variable and complex, and partly because of researchers' biases and failures to plan their studies as carefully as they might.

We do not believe that most or all sex-difference researchers have consciously and purposely set out to do research that is harmful or demeaning to one sex or the other. We do believe, however, that it is hard, if not impossible, for any of us to be aware of all our biases and unquestioned assumptions, and those of us who do research will bring those factors into our research, like it or not. We are all products of our time and culture. No doubt the same applies to us in the writing of this book. So, after reading through the following chapters and honing your critical thinking skills, you may wish to apply them to the arguments and reasoning we use in this book.

A word of warning is in order. Some students have been accustomed to believing that scientists and teachers are always right, and they sometimes find it upsetting to be shown that the so-called experts have often made significant mistakes, unintentional as they may have been. It can feel like the rug of certainty pulled from under us when we start to question what we read or what we are taught. To be sure, we cannot promise to give you new, absolute truths to replace some of the certainty you may lose, but we believe that it is important to know when what we thought was absolute truth is only partial or even nonexistent. Better, we feel, to know the limits of our knowledge than to believe we know more than we actually do.

Furthermore, developing critical thinking skills does *not* leave you with nothing. Instead, it leaves you with a wealth of important abilities which enable you to grapple with research in an active way. And by approaching research with an active mind, you will be in a good position to see which research *is* reasonably done and which researchers try to identify and freely acknowledge their own biases.

When we encounter experimental errors, we should not be surprised; after all, we cannot know anything in this world with absolute certainty. Naturally, error should be minimized, but we can go only so far. The important thing for researchers is to be as accurate as possible but to make sure the conclusions that they draw do not go beyond what the study's method and results, combined with the experimenters' biases, really show.

In the next chapter we shall look briefly at the ways that scientists in an earlier era made claims for their research that went well beyond their methods and results and failed to deal with their biases.

# References

Hochschild, A. (1973). A review of sex role research. In Joan Huber (Ed.), *Changing women in a changing society* (pp. 249–267). Chicago: University of Chicago Press.

Hubbard, R. (1990). *The politics of women's biology.* New Brunswick, NJ: Rutgers University Press.

Hubbard, R., et al. (Eds.). (1982). *Biological woman: The convenient myth.* Cambridge, MA: Schenkman.

CHAPTER
TWO

# A BRIEF HISTORICAL PERSPECTIVE ON SEX-DIFFERENCE RESEARCH[1]

Research on sex differences in behavior has a long history and has aroused intense scientific and public interest in the nineteenth and twentieth centuries. In studying current sex-difference research, knowing something of its historical background is important for several reasons. First, we can learn from the mistakes of those who have gone before us. If we understand the errors researchers have made in the past, it can help us to try to avoid them in our own new research and to progress more efficiently. Second, knowing the history of sex-difference research helps us understand people's attitudes today. Experiments from the last century may sound quaint, naive, and obviously biased to us. We might assume that no researcher today could ever do that kind of research. However, becoming familiar with the faults in those early studies makes it easier to spot the (sometimes more subtle) descendants of such experiments in our own day. Often, we find that studies from a hundred years ago—and the attitudes and prejudices that characterized their experimenters—are really not very different from those of today.

In this chapter, then, we examine some of the influential early research on sex differences, pointing out some common themes, identifying some of the significant and common errors researchers have made, and studying the various assumptions and attitudes displayed by the people who have done the studies and interpreted the results. Then we shall note some parallels in the research of our own era.

---

1. This chapter was extensively based on Catherine Gildiner's 1977 paper, "Science as a political weapon: A study of the nineteenth century sex differences literature." York University, Downsview, Ontario.

## ❖ WHOSE HISTORY IS IT, ANYWAY?

Our culture's modern science was born and reared primarily during the Victorian Age in Europe. At that time and in that place, the people who were the most influential in scientific research were white, middle class or wealthy, and male. The people of that era had been heavily influenced by the Judeo-Christian tradition, which was filled with stories that were used to "prove" women's inferiority to men. At the very beginning of the Bible, for instance, Eve—who symbolizes women in general—is described as having introduced evil (sin) into the world. Although many people might interpret that story differently today, in the Victorian Age this was the most common interpretation (Gildiner, 1977). (In fact, it is worth noting that Eve's "sin" was her desire to eat the fruit from the tree of knowledge. This has been regarded as evidence of women's inferiority or even dangerousness when white, wealthy men control not only religious institutions but also the production of "knowledge" by the institution called Science.)

Religion had for centuries been the authority on human nature. In the nineteenth century the scientific method became a popular way to find out about the world. When people wanted to know about the nature of the world and about the right ways to behave, instead of going directly to their religious leaders for directions about how God wants people to act, they turned increasingly to scientists for answers. Science came to be highly respected, and it has even been said that in some ways it *replaced* religion (Young, 1971).

For the past two centuries, most scientists in the Western hemisphere have come from cultures characterized by certain powerful beliefs, including the belief in the intellectual inferiority of women and of anyone who was not white, and this has profoundly affected the directions research has taken. In fact, most scientists have themselves been members of the privileged class, race, and sex, so it is not surprising that the majority have chosen research questions that have helped to perpetuate the view that members of their group are superior. For example, instead of setting out to investigate *whether* males have superior intellectual abilities, scientists have tended to help maintain the status quo by trying to determine *why* males are intellectually more capable.

## ❖ THE SEARCH FOR PROOF OF WOMEN'S INFERIORITY

### ■ The Great Brain Hunt

Let us look at how scientists in the nineteenth century set about their search for the answer to the question of why women are intellectually inferior to men. As we do this, let us keep in mind that then, as now, researchers may base their research questions on assumptions that they simply believe to be true, without questioning those assumptions—in this case, that women are intellectually inferior. When research is based on an unchallenged assumption it is extremely unlikely that the results of that research will ever lead anyone to question that assumption; for instance, when researchers ask simply *why* it is that women are not very smart, the kinds of studies they design are likely to produce information that seems either to support their assumption or to shed no light on it, but not to disprove it.

One popular notion in the nineteenth century was that women were less intelligent than men because women's brains were smaller than men's. A scientist named George Romanes (1887) claimed to have proven this. Women have smaller heads, he said, therefore they must have smaller brains, and therefore they are less intelligent. Those who wished to believe in females' inferiority thus believed that data had been found to explain it. Rarely did anyone even raise such questions as, "If a woman had a very large head, would we say she is smarter than most men?" Romanes's claim was eventually discredited (Gildiner, 1977).

The work of Romanes illustrates yet another important point: When "data" seem to confirm what is already believed, not only is the assumption underlying the research hardly ever questioned but also people go on to construct elaborate theories based on that assumption and those data. For instance, as a result of Romanes's conclusions, other writers then went on to say that women's lesser intelligence was actually necessary for the survival of the human species, since women—having no intellectual interests—would be free to devote their energies exclusively to bearing and raising children (Mobius, 1901). Then, as with many theories, a considerable number of scientists and laypeople became so fascinated by the survival theory about sex differences in intelligence that they were even *less* likely to devote their energies to going back to Romanes's study and thinking critically about how he conducted it and the merits of his underlying assumption. This process continues today, as we describe in Chapter 4, on spatial abilities.

The long life of beliefs based on Romanes' research *after* the research had been discredited reflects another characteristic of the way people treat scientists' claims about their research: Many scientists and laypeople (and, today, the media) become intensely interested in an issue, believe a report of some bit of research about that issue, and then lose interest in it (Davidson, 1991). If, later on, the research they had read about is discredited, they may have become so accustomed to believing in that early research that they do not invest the mental and emotional energy necessary to revise their belief. This is particularly true when the earlier research seems to confirm what they, for their own personal and/or political reasons, *wanted* to believe. In this way, although the claims about brain size determining sex differences in intelligence were later discredited, many people continued to believe both in females' intellectual inferiority and in Mobius's "explanation" of the survival value of that inferiority.

Some researchers, however, rather than clinging to belief in the Romanes research, clung to their basic assumption about the intellectual inferiority of females but decided it would be important to find out where, other than in simple brain size, that inferiority was based. There then followed decades of what may seem to us today to be amusingly misguided experiments—

researchers comparing one aspect or segment after another in the brains of the two sexes, desperately seeking difference.

After most people gave up on believing that bigger brains were better, some scientists, still assuming women were the less intelligent sex, proposed that the sex difference might be *relative* brain size, that is, the size of the brain relative to the size of the body. But this effort backfired—relative to body size, it was learned, women's brains were actually *larger* than men's.

So, researchers gave up on the whole-brain theories, but the quest continued. If it wasn't due to the size of the whole brain, scientists speculated, perhaps there was a difference in the size of one *part* of the brain, whichever part might be the crucial seat of intelligence. This, too, turned out to be a fruitless direction for the researchers' purposes, however. Scientists checked one segment—or lobe—of the brain after another, expecting that each part would be larger in men than in women. In no case was the expectation borne out.

Today, we might think that such studies are no longer done, especially since it is well known that chemical and electrical changes, not sheer volume and weight, are the keys to brain functioning. Furthermore, it is now known that intelligence does not lie in only one site in the brain. Rather, each of a vast number of different parts of the brain is related to one or more of a vast number of intellectual abilities. However, in 1987, Dr. Ruth Bleier told an important story to the American Association for the Advancement of Science. She described a piece of research that had been published in the highly respected journal *Science* (deLacoste-Utamsing & Holloway, 1982), in which it was claimed that the *splenium,* the back part of the membrane which separates the two hemispheres of the human brain, was bigger in females than in males. The authors of the study suggested that this sex difference might explain females' supposedly inferior spatial abilities (see Chapter 4 for a detailed discussion of this topic). Bleier and her colleagues carefully read that study and found that it was filled with major flaws, not the least of which was that only nine males' and only five females' brains had been studied. As part of her presentation, she showed a slide on which pictures of the splenium from a number of males were displayed in one column, and those from a number of females in the other. She asked the audience to determine by looking which were the males' and which were the females', or which column had clearly larger segments. It was clearly impossible to tell from simply looking at them. Bleier explained that she and her colleagues then looked at the spleniums from a much larger number of people of both sexes, had the segments carefully and objectively measured, and found no sex difference at all. When they submitted their article about this work to *Science* magazine, it was turned down on the grounds that it was too "political."

This illustrates another important point: Historically, whether in the nineteenth century or in our own time, research that supports the beliefs of the people in power is likely to be readily and unquestioningly accepted as legitimate research; however, research that might lead people to question those beliefs is scrutinized for methodological flaws and is dismissed as "motivated by political aims." Of course, research that supports the status quo may also be motivated by political aims, but that does not tend to be recognized, because those who control the political and scientific arenas simply feel that it confirms what they already "knew" to be true.

During the nineteenth century, as one by one the parts of the brain were found not to differ in females and males, scientists reached further to try to find the physical location of what they believed to be males' superior intelligence. For instance, they measured the length of the spinal cord, putting together convoluted explanations for how a sex difference in spinal cord length might be related to intelligence. And this was done in all seriousness.

In this research enterprise, scientists not only measured parts of the body but also administered various tests to people of both sexes. When females performed better than males on such tests, it seems that the researchers had to find some way to transform that information into further "proof" of males' superiority (Caplan, 1989). Romanes (1887), for instance, conducted a study in which he found that women could read faster and more accurately than men. Instead of simply concluding that women could read faster and more accurately than men—or even that, in this respect, women might be more intelligent than men—two prominent scientists of the era accounted for the sex difference by saying that the ability to read is coupled with the ability to lie, and women are better liars than men (Lombroso & Ferrero, quoted by Ellis, 1934). In this way, a finding of a female superiority in a skill was transformed into evidence of females' moral inferiority.

Not only data-gathering research but also theories were powerful tools in the nineteenth century for justifying the privileged positions of well-to-do, white males. We shall now look at what was probably the most influential of those theories.


### ■ Social Darwinism

A major theory that was used to "explain" women's intellectual inferiority is *Social Darwinism,* using Charles Darwin's claim that, as species evolve, the individual animals and humans that survive tend to be those that are the best suited to their environments. This was his concept of *survival of the fittest.* Social Darwinists reasoned that, therefore, whatever survives, including social and political structures, individuals, and aspects of human personality, must be the fittest. Thus, they said, what exists today must be the best possible state of things.

Since women were already considered less intelligent than men, it was argued that such a sex difference was necessary for the survival of the species (for instance, so that women could put all of their energy into bearing and raising children). Similar reasoning was used to justify a myriad of factors that had actually been imposed by society, not determined by evolution. For instance, the intense social pressure on women to behave passively did tend to make many women rather passive. But Social Darwinists then claimed that this was a biologically based trait, necessary for encouraging women's sexual passivity and receptivity, so that they would become pregnant and thereby help the species to survive.

Also related to Social Darwinism was the *maternal instinct* theory, according to which women have an innate desire to take care of children, while men do not. Therefore, goes the theory, men can develop other abilities, like intelligence and perseverance, while women must concentrate on nurturing and protecting. Even if there is some maternal instinct in human females, that would hardly explain women's "lesser intelligence." In fact, certain intellectual capacities are enormously helpful in making women (or men, for that matter) better nurturers, protectors, and conveyors to the young of information that can help them survive and flourish (Ruddick, 1989).

Still another theoretical tack related to Darwinism was a notion called *morphological infantilism.* Proposed by Darwin, it is the idea that women, being smaller than men, are morphologically (physically) more like infants and children than are men. Some Victorian theorists speculated that, therefore, women are less intelligent than men but more intelligent than infants and children. This is equivalent to saying that men must be more like gorillas than are women, because men are hairier: It might even be valid, but what reason is there to believe it? The reason for using the notion of morphological infantilism to "explain" women's allegedly inferior intellectual capacity was, again, to justify depriving women of legal, economic, and political power. The Social Darwinists who promoted morphological infantilism as applied to women used the same notion for keeping Whites in power over Blacks. Black people, they argued, are physically more similar to apes than are white people and are therefore less intelligent. Clearly, Black women were the group most demeaned by this sexist and racist theory.

Morphological infantilism and other Social Darwinist theories might seem to be another of the quaint nineteenth-century theories that seem shockingly prejudiced as well as groundless to us today. But in our own era, Philippe Rushton (1989) has attracted wide media coverage with his claims that such characteristics as brain size and numbers of offspring prove that "Orientals" are more advanced on the evolutionary scale than Whites, and Blacks are less advanced than both. Two of the key components in Rushton's argument are that the number of offspring a woman produces and the duration of her pregnancies are signs of her place on the scales of intelligence and evolutionary advancement. Thus, women's bodies again become a prime focus for arguments about which humans are inferior to which others. Although his work has been criticized in great detail for its extremely poor methodology and its racist and sexist qualities, some people nevertheless want to believe he is right.

## ❖ SUMMARY OF SOME PROBLEMATIC PATTERNS

In this chapter, we identified some of the problematic patterns of scientists' behavior in studies of the history of research that persist even today. These include:

1. beginning with a biased assumption (e.g., that males are more intelligent than females)

2. failing to question the assumption(s) underlying the research (e.g., failing to question whether the predominance of males in high academic and political positions is proof of males' greater intelligence)

3. asking research questions based on that assumption (e.g., "Is men's greater intelligence due to their bigger brains?")

4. when results of a study do not support the assumption, continuing to avoid questioning the assumption (e.g., if men's brains turn out not to be larger than women's, relative to their body sizes, then not questioning whether men are more intelligent)

5. misinterpreting research results that seem to contradict the assumption. (Thus, what had been considered a desirable characteristic—such as reading quickly—is portrayed as an undesirable one, or one that *leads to* trouble)

6. failing to question the evidence for, the logic of, and the damaging consequences of theories

Our predecessors in the history of research on sex differences certainly made major—and often damaging and oppressive—errors in conducting, interpreting, and theorizing about their investigations. That historical perspective is helpful to keep in mind as we turn in the next chapter to some specific methodological errors often made by researchers and then move in the following chapters to an examination of the research on particular topics.

# References

Bleier, R. (1987, February). *Sex-differences research in the neurosciences.* Paper presented at the symposium on Bias in Sex-differences Research, American Association for the Advancement of Science Annual Meeting, Chicago.

Caplan, P. J. (1989). *Don't blame mother: Mending the mother-daughter relationship.* New York: Harper & Row.

Davidson, K. (1991, January 20). Nature vs. nurture. *San Francisco Examiner Image.* pp. 10–17.

deLacoste-Utamsing, C., & Holloway, R. L. (1982). Sexual dimorphism in the human corpus callosum. *Science, 216,* 1431–1432.

Ellis, H. (1934). *Man and woman: A study of secondary and tertiary sexual characteristics.* Cambridge, MA: The Riverside Press.

Gildiner, C. (1977). *Science as a political weapon: A study of the nineteenth century sex differences literature.* Psychology Department, York University, Downsview, Ontario.

Mobius, P. J. (A. McCorn, trans.) (1901). The physiological mental weakness of women. *Alienist and Neurologist, 22,* 624–642.

Romanes, G. J. (1887). Mental differences between men and women. *Nineteenth Century, 21,* 654–672.

Ruddick, S. (1989). *Maternal thinking: Toward a politics of peace.* Boston: Beacon.

Rushton, J. P. (1989, January). *Evolutionary biology and heritable traits (with reference to Oriental-White-Black differences).* Paper prepared for presentation at American Association for the Advancement of Science convention, San Francisco.

Young, R. M. (1971). Evolutionary biology and ideology: Then and now. *Science Studies, 1,* 177–206.

**CHAPTER THREE**

# USING SCIENTIFIC METHOD TO STUDY SEX AND GENDER

Science is a method of asking questions and trying to find the answers. There are many ways to ask a question. As noted in Chapter 2, many centuries ago, people looked to religion for answers to their questions. They went to religious leaders or studied legends for explanations and for the truth. Nowadays, most people believe that scientists are the truth-knowers, and as a result, many people have great respect for the scientific method. Unfortunately, it is extremely hard to do flawless research about human behavior, so it is hard for scientists to find the Truth. In this chapter, we look at some of the most common kinds of errors scientists make in conducting their research, errors which make it difficult to judge how close to real knowledge their research has brought them.

The term *scientific method* is defined in the *New Webster's Dictionary of the English Language* as a research method involving the definition of a problem and the drafting and empirical testing of the hypotheses by gathering data. In other words, the scientific method is a way to conduct research to find out about something by using a plan. It is commonly believed that the scientific method is an objective way to find the truth—that it is not affected by scientists' beliefs, feelings, or biases. The scientific method is said to produce results that are reliable. If a scientific experiment is conducted well, then the results can be replicated or reproduced in another study, and this suggests that such results are true. If the results are not reproducible, then how can we tell which set of results is closer to the truth? A key feature of the scientific method is the careful documentation of *every* step of the procedure, so that *anyone* can reproduce the experiments to test the original results.

In reality, however, very few scientific studies are ideal; many things can go wrong and thus give a distorted picture of the topic being studied. In the

**19**

area of research on sex and gender, research errors leading to distortions have been extremely common; as a result, we have often seen a very inaccurate picture of the similarities and differences between the sexes. It has been like looking in a curved mirror. In each of Chapters 4 through 11, some of the most important research mistakes related to particular topics are described.

We shall introduce you to some very common methodological errors so that they will be familiar to you by the time you reach the specific topic chapters. (We will not describe some of the more technical errors or those involving statistics, however; for some excellent sources of more information on this topic, please see the Suggested Readings section at the end of this book.) We hope that you will not feel so disheartened after reading about sources of error that you will want to ignore all research forever. It is our hope that with knowledge about common sources of error, you will be able to take into account the errors you find before you draw conclusions about a study. In other words, it is not always necessary to conclude that a study is worthless because it is not perfect, but your knowledge of its limitations should help you decide how to interpret it, the extent to which you can rely on its data, how important it is, and so on. Problems arise not so much because experiments are biased but because researchers and laypeople do not take those errors and biases into account in evaluating them. The interpretation of a study should take *every* aspect of the experiment—*including its limitations*—into consideration.

For purposes of illustration, we shall here use sex differences in strength as an example. In order to understand what can go wrong in using the scientific method, let us follow the steps of a scientific study.

## ❖ 1. CHOOSING WHAT TO STUDY

The first step in *any* scientific study is to decide what you want to find out. Scientists don't randomly choose what they study. Scientists are human and tend to study what interests them. Often, this means that they have strong needs to prove that something is true or false, and those needs can affect the way they ask the research question: for instance, they might study the question "Why are women so weak?" rather than "Under what circumstances can people become as strong as possible?" As noted earlier, a scientist may or may not be aware of these needs, and probably most do not purposely bring their biases into their research planning. But whether these biases and motives are conscious or not, and whether they are intentionally or unintentionally brought into the activity of choosing a research question, this is *very* different from the picture of the objective scientist. Most scientists have beliefs, hypotheses or predictions about the outcomes of their studies; as we shall see later, the researcher's beliefs and predictions can heavily influence the outcome of the study.

# ❖ 2. DETERMINING EXACTLY WHAT YOU'RE LOOKING FOR

You must define what you are looking for. This is extremely important. For example, if a researcher set out to explore sex differences in something we'll call *flugenransk,* but didn't define it, you would have absolutely no idea whether or not the study proved that the sexes differed in *flugenransk.* Without a clear and adequate definition, you cannot be sure that the tests you've chosen actually measure what you are trying to measure. Let's say that a researcher, Dr. Wright, decides to study sex differences in strength. There is more than one meaning of the word *strength.* One is physical ability, another is mental power, another is endurance (physical or mental), and another refers to smell or taste. Maybe Dr. Wright is trying to study sex differences in physical ability, or physical endurance, or mental ability, or emotional resilience, or perhaps she is trying to test whether women or men emit a stronger odor after exercise. Most likely she intends to study one of the earlier items on the list, but it is unscientific and inefficient not to specify that precisely.

With more complicated concepts, precise definitions are even more crucial. For instance, if you are studying "intelligence," you must say *exactly* what you mean by intelligence, because it has been defined in many ways, which include an astonishing variety of abilities (such as the ability to take in information, the ability to learn concepts, the ability to memorize, the ability to re-create with a pen and paper exactly what you see, etc.). If we don't know exactly how a researcher is defining a concept, we simply don't know what is proven by the results of the research.

Furthermore, to answer a scientific question, we must have a clear and precise question so that it can be answered with clarity and precision. There are a number of different questions Dr. Wright could be asking about sex differences in strength, for example, "Are there sex differences in strength?" or "Under what conditions are sex differences in strength the greatest?" or "What conditions cause sex differences in strength to disappear?" or "Are there sex differences in *every* kind of strength?" If she doesn't state her question accurately, the same problem arises as with failing to state the precise definition: She can't tell if she is actually testing her question, and she won't know if she was successful.

# ❖ 3. DESIGNING THE RESEARCH

The third step is to design some kind of method for gathering relevant information. Many things can go wrong here.

First, *the method must relate back to the research questions or hypotheses and/or theories on which the study is based.* If they don't, your conclusion will be irrelevant to your hypotheses. To take an extreme example, let's say that

Dr. Wright hypothesizes that males will be physically stronger than females, and she uses the following method:

1. She has each member of a group of people eat an apple.

2. She asks each one if they enjoyed eating the apple.

No matter what her results are, they're irrelevant, because they have nothing to do with her hypothesis about strength. Even if the males *did* enjoy the apple more than the females did, it wouldn't tell us anything about their physical strength. Of course, errors in research methods are usually much more subtle, but you must be careful to ensure that your method relates to your hypotheses.

Second, *certain methodological errors can skew the results.* Some of these can appear in any methods, while others are inherent only in certain *kinds* of methods. Following are some examples:

**1. Experimenter Bias.** Experimenter bias involves the intrusion of the researcher's beliefs or hopes into the actual study. Experimenter bias in the plan of a study can lead to very distorted results. For instance, suppose Dr. Wright believes and hypothesizes that males are physically stronger than females. That might lead her to test her hypothesis by comparing the number of males who have cargo-loading jobs to the number of females in such jobs. She would then be ignoring the fact that most of the carrying of toddlers and groceries (which also requires great physical strength) is done by females. In any experiment, it is almost impossible to eliminate bias completely. Therefore, it is important both to acknowledge that and to keep trying to be as objective as possible.

**2. Errors in Cross-Sectional Research.** If you want to measure change over time, there are two practical ways to go about it, each of which is problematic. One of these is *cross-sectional* research, which involves testing people from different age groups at the same time. Suppose Dr. Wright wants to find out whether physical strength diminishes more with age in males or in females. Using a cross-sectional approach, she tests females and males from different age groups (e.g., 10- to 20-year-olds, 21- to 30-year-olds, and so on) and notes the changes for each sex across the age range. Suppose that she finds that the older males are weaker than the younger ones but for females, strength doesn't vary from one age group to another. She would not be justified in concluding that males grow weaker over time until she could prove that the males of different ages had all had the same experiences at the same times in their lives. For instance, perhaps the teenage males in her study are required by a new Board of Education rule to take more stringent physical education courses than the men now in their twenties were required to take as teenagers. If that difference in life history distinguished men in the different age groups from each other, then we would not necessarily expect that the current teenagers will be as weak as the current 20-year-olds when the teenagers reach their twenties. Therefore, it would be wrong to conclude that each man grows weaker as he grows older.

**3. Errors in Longitudinal Research.** The other way to measure change over time is by using the *longitudinal* method, which involves measuring the same people several times as they grow older. For instance, instead of the cross-sectional method, Dr. Wright might decide to measure the individual strength of members of a group several times over a period of 10 years. She might find that as her subjects become older, the females seem to lose more strength than the males. She might conclude that, as people get older, women tend to lose their strength faster than men. However, life history can confuse the issue here, too. What if, during the course of the study, it becomes fashionable for women to appear as slim and unmuscular as possible? Then, some women would probably exercise less and, therefore, their strength would diminish from lack of use, not from age. It is extremely difficult, with this kind of method, to determine whether a pattern changed because the people grew older or because some other factor was involved.

**4. Pretest/Posttest.** Often, researchers will want to explore the effect of a certain type of treatment on a group of people. One method commonly used is the pretest/posttest method, in which the subjects are given a certain test before and after the treatment. If their test scores change, it is assumed to be due to the treatment. The problem with this method is similar to that for a longitudinal study, because even if there *is* a difference in the scores for the two tests, in most circumstances it is extremely difficult to be sure that the *treatment*, rather than some other factor, led to the change. For instance, suppose Dr. Wright decided to study whether there is a sex difference in the body's ability to become stronger from increased exercise. One way to test for this might be to measure the difference between people's strength before and after two months of intensive weight training. The problem is that something that happened during the two months could influence the outcome. What if, at that time, an advertisement appeared, encouraging men to take steroids? Then, the steroids would increase the men's ability to become stronger but would not affect the women. If Dr. Wright were unaware that the advertisement had appeared, she could not take its effects into account in interpreting the results of the research and might mistakenly conclude that men become stronger from exercise than women do. It is next to impossible to make sure that between a pre- and a posttest nothing will happen except what the researcher wants to change. This is less problematic when the time between the two tests is short.

**5. Maturation:** Maturation of the people being studied can introduce confusion. Consider the pretest/posttest example. What if people just change over time? What if, as time goes by, men just get stronger faster than women, naturally, even *without* the extra exercise? To determine whether extra exercise or maturation led to the result, the researcher needs to use a *control* group as well as the *experimental* group. She would simply test the control group at the beginning and the end of the week during which members of the experi-

mental group do extra exercise. Any difference between the control and experimental groups is then assumed to be due to the extra exercise.

**6. Test/Retest:** There is yet another problem with the pretest/posttest
method, but it usually applies to a somewhat more complicated kind of test. It
has been shown that people tend to do better the second time they take a test
than the first time. This may be because they get used to the format of the test,
they don't waste as much time figuring out how to do the test, or they simply
become used to the test and are therefore less anxious. No matter what the
reason actually is, it is important to know that people tend to do better the
second time they take a test. So, if an experimental group scores higher on a
posttest than a pretest, it may be due to the second-test effect instead of the
experimental treatment (such as extra exercise or training). One way of getting
around this problem is to use a control group (i.e., these people would take
the test and retest *without* receiving the training). Then, any test/retest effect
would be seen in the controls.

**7. Order Effect.** Often, researchers study how a group of factors affects a
group of people. However, the order in which the people are exposed to the
factors can affect the outcome of the study. For instance, say Dr. Wright
designs a complex test of physical strength, involving almost every muscle in
the human body, in order to be able to test for *overall* strength. If she always
started each subject with pushups and then situps, the outcome could be different than if she reversed the order. What if, for example, males are better at
pushups than situps, and women are better at situps? Then, the women would
be more tired after having had to do the difficult pushups and would have less
energy for the easier situps, while the men would have plenty of energy for
the task that is harder for them. It is always necessary to vary the order of
items in a study to counteract this effect.

## ❖ 4. CARRYING OUT THE STUDY

As you can see by now, it is virtually impossible to develop a perfect research
method. This is especially true for research in psychology, because it's much
harder to do totally controlled experiments on human behavior than on a
chemical in a test tube, for example. So if a method *seems* perfect, beware—
there may well be some hidden problematic factors. But even if it *were* possible to *design* a perfect study, a great deal can go wrong as the researcher car-
ries out the research. Descriptions of some of these pitfalls follow. Although
many of the mistakes will seem glaringly obvious, the fact is that they are frequently made and not accounted for.

**1. Accuracy of the Instrument.** If the instruments used are not very
accurate, the results will also not be very accurate. For instance, if Dr. Wright
decides to measure her research participants' strength by seeing how hard they
can push down on a scale, if she uses a scale that is normally used to measure

the mass of a horse, then she will find very little difference among her subjects, whereas if she uses a more sensitive scale, she will be able to measure the differences more accurately. This principle does not apply only to physical instruments; for example, if a math test does not include math problems of a wide variety of types and of degrees of difficulty, the researcher cannot make valid claims about what the results show about sex differences in math performance.

2. **"Mortality."** If a researcher starts out with a certain number of participants in an experiment, but some drop out (for whatever reason), this could seriously affect the results. This dropout is called participant "mortality," regardless of the reasons for the dropout. For instance, suppose Dr. Wright decides to study the effect of extra exercise on the strength of males versus that of females. Her method is to develop a weight-training program for all the participants and then to measure changes in strength. Now suppose that one-third of the females drop out of the experiment. What if those females dropped out because the weight-training program was too hard for them? These people could be the weaker ones, who might have shown more improvement in strength than the others. Dropout often occurs for some significant reason that distorts the results in a systematic way. Therefore, any mortality at all in a study should make you think twice about accepting the results.

3. **Self-reported Observations.** Sometimes a researcher bases a study on participants' reports or observations. Suppose Dr. Wright decides to measure sex differences in strength by asking people how much weight they can lift. Asking them might seem like a good way to determine how much weight they can lift, but the results from the experiment still won't be very accurate. Maybe some subjects don't like to admit that they're not strong. If males are more embarrassed about seeming weak than are females, then the males would appear to be stronger than they were. Depending on the purpose of the research, self-reported observations may give the most accurate or relevant information, but care must be used in interpreting them. It is too easy to make a mistake. You must consider all possible reasons that researchers might distort or fudge their results (intentionally or unintentionally).

4. **The Participants Know Too Much.** Sometimes the participants figure out why they are being tested, and as a result, they—purposely or unintentionally—act differently, thereby changing the outcome. Other times, they *think* they know what the researcher is looking for but they are wrong. As a result, they also act differently and skew the results. And although occasionally researchers will ask the participants, after the experiment, how much they had known, usually that does not happen.

5. **Sampling Error.** Often it is impossible to test *everyone* in a group of people you wish to study. Therefore, you may need to test only a *sample* of the total population and *assume* that they will probably perform roughly the same as the whole population. For instance, if Dr. Wright wanted to find the difference in strength between the average woman and the average man, she couldn't *possibly* test *all* the men and women in existence. Instead, she might

choose five people of each sex at random, test them, and assume that they represent the general population. But what if they *don't* represent the total population? What if she just *happened* to pick the five strongest men in the world? Or what if she happened to pick five women, each of whom is a full-time mother or has a demanding paid job and has no time for exercise? Then, her results wouldn't accurately represent all women and men. What if she used a hundred people instead? The chances that *they* accurately represent the total population would be higher, and therefore, her results would probably be more accurate. If she used a million people, they would most likely provide an even more accurate estimate. In summary, if you don't test the whole population, you can't be absolutely certain that your results are accurate, but the larger the sample, the more accurate your results are likely to be.

**6. Experimenter Bias.** If Dr. Wright expects certain results and is the person who is doing the actual data gathering, then she may tend to make errors that conform to her expectations. For instance, if she is measuring how many kilograms of potatoes people can lift, and she assumes that men can lift heavier loads of potatoes than women can, consider what may happen when it comes time for her to weigh the potatoes. As she weighs a sack of potatoes lifted by a woman and she thinks the scale may read either 39 or 40 kilograms, her expectations may lead her to record the weight as 39—and to do the reverse if she were weighing the same sackful for a man. Sometimes it is possible to avoid this problem by altering the design of the experiment slightly—for instance, she might ask someone else (who doesn't know the sex of weight lifter) to read the scales.

## ❖ 5. INTERPRETING THE RESULTS

Consider the story about a misguided fellow trying to teach his students about interpreting scientific research. He showed his students a normal frog and said, "Jump!" to the frog. It jumped. Then, demonstrating how one records scientific observations, he wrote on the blackboard, "Frog with four legs jumps." He then cut off one of the frog's legs and said, "Jump!" It jumped—less gracefully, of course. This time he wrote on the board, "Frog with three legs jumps." He cut off a second of the frog's legs, then a third, and after each time gave the same command. Each time the frog jumped, although more awkwardly each time. Accordingly, he wrote on the board the lines "Frog with two legs jumps" and "Frog with one leg jumps." Finally, he cut off the fourth leg and said, "Jump!" When the frog failed to jump, the teacher instructed the students: "Frog with no legs becomes deaf!"

The final step in any scientific study is interpreting the results. In many ways, this is the most important step. If there were any possible sources of error in the study, here is where they must be reported. The researcher must take into account *every* detail of the study and come up with an interpretation related to what *actually* happened. There are several ways this might *not* come about:

**1. Cause and Effect Problems.** If one event, A, was found to happen only when another event, B, happened, you might conclude that B caused A or that A caused B. These are valid *possibilities*, but you must always remember that there is a third possibility: that a further event, C, might have caused *both* A and B. For example, suppose that Dr. Wright observed that women who ate healthier foods were stronger that women who did not. She might conclude that the type of food women eat affects their strength, or that being strong causes women to eat healthier food, but there is a third possibility—that an external event (e.g., the women's attitude about general health) affects both their strength and their diet. She must take into account all three possibilities.

**2. Different Interpretations.** There are usually many different ways to interpret any result. This doesn't mean necessarily that *all* of them are right or that *none* of them is right. It just means that if you find certain results and think of *one* way to interpret them, you must remember that it isn't necessarily the *only* reasonable way. For instance, suppose Dr. Wright sets up an experiment in which women and men are given a very heavy weight and a skateboard and are told that they must transport the weight a certain distance. Now suppose that most of the women use the skateboard to help them move the weight, while most of the men don't use the skateboard. Dr. Wright might conclude that the men are stronger, that the women just aren't strong enough to move the weight without the help of the skateboard. Or, she might conclude that the women are lazier than the men. Or, she might believe that the men's need to be macho would prevent them from using the skateboard. Or, she might say that the men have weaker eyes and don't notice that the skateboard is there. Or, she might decide that the men aren't smart enough to figure out how to use the skateboard to make the chore easier for them. In other words, no matter what we conclude from this experiment, all we can *really* be sure of is that more of the women used the skateboard than the men. We can make up interpretations, but we must remember that the *real* reason for the results could easily be something that has never occurred to us.

## ❖ 6. META-ANALYSIS: COMBINING STUDIES

An increasingly popular technique is *meta-analysis*, which is a way of using statistical methods to combine a large number of studies and analyzing their results as a group. Some people have claimed that this is useful, because, for example, you need not ignore studies that were conducted on a very small number of people. Some also say that, although Study A may suffer from Methodological Problem X, Study B from Problem Y, and so on, if you combine many studies, their good parts probably tell something important. Although there are some mathematical formulas that can help to minimize the effects of the problems, if we combine many studies, each of which is flawed in some ways we know about and probably in others we haven't yet recognized, then several problems arise:

1. It is hard to know whether the problems cancel each other out or just add up to more problems.

2. Because the statistics are fairly sophisticated, we may assume that they will yield some important truth. But both simple and sophisticated mistakes can be made using sophisticated techniques.

3. As we have seen in this chapter, even *defining* what we are studying and choosing the *ways* to study it can be difficult. If each study (or most) in a meta-analysis suffers from some lack of clarity of definition, if different ways are used for measuring the behavior, or if somewhat different forms of behavior were studied, then we are combining apples, oranges, walnuts, and maybe ironing boards! It doesn't make logical sense to analyze such a mixture as though the elements were nearly the same.

Now you are familiar with many of the research problems that plague the study of sex and gender. In the following chapters, you will see how these and other kinds of problems arise in the research and lead to mistaken impressions about people of both sexes. Remember that our aim in this book is to focus on the limitations of research, the factors that should make us slow to accept scientists' claims about their studies. But that does not mean that no research is ever helpful in moving us toward important knowledge. For instance, although longitudinal studies have the kinds of drawbacks we have noted, if they are carefully planned, if the data are appropriately analyzed, and if the results are responsibly interpreted, they can provide useful information (such as the relationship between certain food elements and disease). Sometimes, there is no substitute for research in answering important questions. But these questions must be carefully considered, and the research should be conducted with an acute awareness of its limitations.

# CHAPTER FOUR

# SEX DIFFERENCES IN SPATIAL ABILITIES[1]

**"W**omen can't read road maps. They're just no good at doing spatial tasks," people often say. The claim that females have inferior spatial abilities is usually based on such tests as map-reading, maze-drawing, and picturing how block structures would look if they were turned around. The belief in this alleged inferiority has been used to justify keeping girls and women out of advanced science and mathematics classes and out of such careers as engineering, scientific research, architecture, building construction, various forms of navigation including piloting aircraft, and map development and design.

Especially when a claim about sex differences has such extensive impact on people's education and career tracks, it is important to look carefully at whether that claim has any basis in fact. To consider the topic of sex differences in spatial abilities, we shall be asking three sets of questions:

1. What are spatial abilities?

2. *Are* there sex differences in spatial abilities? If so, how significant are they?

3. Why have people believed that there are such big differences in these abilities?

## ❖ WHAT ARE SPATIAL ABILITIES?

Trying to define and describe spatial abilities is not like trying to define and describe a table. If five people are sitting at a table, they can all agree that

1. Portions of this chapter were excerpted from Paula J. Caplan, Gael M. MacPherson, and Patricia Tobin, "Do sex-related differences in spatial abilities exist? A multilevel critique with new data," *American Psychologist, 40* (1985), 786–799.

they are sitting at a wooden piece of furniture that has four legs and a horizontal top. *Table* is something which clearly exists and can be easily identified by anyone. The concept of *spatial abilities* is a totally different matter: If you ask five so-called "experts" how they define or identify spatial abilities, you will probably get five somewhat different definitions, and within each definition you will likely get vague or confusing terms.

Let us look closely at some examples of these definitions and then think about what we learn from them. We shall go into a great deal of detail, because in order to know what we are dealing with when we talk about spatial abilities, we must first determine whether we even know what spatial abilities are.

Harris (1978) has written:

> Spatial ability has been variously defined: "to move, turn, twist, or rotate an object or objects and to recognize a new appearance or position after the prescribed manipulation has been performed" (Guilford, 1947); "to recognize the identity of an object when it is seen from different angles" (Thurstone, 1950); "to think about those spatial relations in which the body orientation of the observer is an essential part of the problem" (Thurstone, 1950); "to perceive spatial patterns accurately and to compare them with each other" (French, 1951). Each characterization implies mental imagery, but of a distinctly kinetic rather than a static kind. (p. 405)

Lips, Myers, and Colwill (1978) wrote: "Spatial abilities are those that enable a person to locate an object in space, mentally rearrange objects, recognize shapes, and so on. This broad class of abilities is tested using tasks such as block design, jigsaw puzzles, mazes, and matching forms" (p. 156).

Now, what can we say about these definitions? Two of the three features of spatial abilities as defined by Lips et al. do *not* involve mental rearrangement or rotation, which was at the core of the definitions Harris considered. Their use of the phrase "and so on" adds nothing that helps us define or identify spatial abilities. Maccoby and Jacklin (1974) reported that "spatial ability, even more than verbal or quantitative ability, is difficult to define" (p. 91). They then, however, listed a host of factors that they said might be included in spatial ability(ies). As possible components they cited such skills as identifying which direction a sound came from, realizing that an object remains the same size even though it looks smaller when far away, recognizing an object by touch even when it has been turned around, and choosing which shapes can be turned around and fitted together to form a specified figure. They went on to consider the following skills as possible further components: the abilities to say how one part of a gear system moves when you turn another part in the system; to say how many sides of a pile of blocks someone can see from a perspective different from your own; to perform the Block Design subtest on the most frequently used intelligence test for children; and accurately to do mazes, certain kinds of puzzles, and two tests called the Embedded Figures Test (in which one tries to identify certain figures within a design made up of other figures) and the Rod-and-Frame Test (RFT; in which one is asked to sit in a chair whose position can be changed, to look at a tilted picture frame, and then to adjust a rod so that it remains straight). Various other authors (such as Cooper & Shepard, 1973; Harshman, Hampson, & Berenbaum, 1983) have attempted to analyze the term *spatial abilities* into its components and have come up with other, somewhat different lists.

In the midst of this perplexing array of approaches to analyzing the general term *spatial abilities* into its possible components, the term *spatial visualization* is often proposed as one component. It seems to mean trying to picture something, but as MacFarlane-Smith (1964) has written, no practical definition of spatial *visualization* has been generally accepted. That was true when MacFarlane-Smith's article was published in 1964, and it remains true today.

When different researchers use different definitions and different tests but all claim to be measuring something called *spatial abilities,* and when each research team then gets a different result, it looks as though there are totally conflicting findings about the same ability or set of abilities. In fact, however, each team is studying a different ability or set of abilities.

Since we know that that happens, we ought to realize that there is no way we can conclude on the basis of these kinds of research that "males are better than females on spatial tasks." However, that is exactly what has been claimed. Why is that? Historically, here is what has tended to happen. Research Team A decided to examine sex differences in spatial ability, chose Test 1 as what seemed to them to be a reasonable test of spatial ability, and found that boys did better. Research Team B decided to examine spatial ability using Test 2 and found no sex difference. Research Team C chose Test 3 of "spatial ability" and found that males did slightly better at some ages but not at all ages. Reviewers have tended to summarize results A, B, and C as "Males are better spatially than females," and experimental results that are not consistent with that summary (like those of Research Team B) have been easily overlooked.

Because of these problems with definitions, some tests have been called spatial abilities tests even though they appear to have little or nothing to do with what most people would consider to be *spatial abilities* (Caplan, MacPherson, & Tobin, 1985). For some tests of *spatial abilities* the score is determined more by nonspatial than by spatial factors. For example, the Rod and Frame Test is sometimes claimed to be a test of spatial abilities, but it has been suggested (Sherman, 1978) that scores on this test may be importantly affected by assertiveness and by fear or uneasiness (the latter because the test has often been given to females by male experimenters in a darkened room). Furthermore, although it is claimed that males perform better than females on the RFT, when a human figure is used in this test instead of an abstract rod, no sex difference in performance appears, and when the participants are told the RFT is a test of empathy or ability to understand how other people feel, females perform better (Naditch, 1976).

Keeping in mind the fact that there is so much confusion about whether there is such a thing as *spatial ability*—and if there is, whether it is one ability or many—let us now look at the magnitude of the alleged sex differences in this research.

## ❖ EXTENT OF SEX DIFFERENCES

To hear many educators and laypeople talk, one would think that, whatever spatial abilities might be, males are substantially superior in that arena. However, most studies actually yield no difference at all. Furthermore, when sex differences have appeared, they have had the following characteristics:

1. They are small (Kimball, 1981).

2. The overlap in males' and females' scores is great (Kimball, 1981).

3. The differences are unreliable, so that when a test is given several times, sometimes a sex difference appears and sometimes it does not (Annett, 1980; Foley & Cohen, 1984).

4. When a sex difference appears, it is almost always around or after adolescence (Caplan et al., 1985).

5. Given the huge sex differences in socialization related to "spatial abilities"—such as children learning early that girls cannot read maps, do math and science, estimate distances, and so on—it is amazing that "spatial abilities" tests do not yield enormous, reliable, lifelong differences (Caplan et al., 1985).

Several of these points deserve further discussion. For instance, in regard to #1, the small size of sex differences when differences do appear, Hyde (1981) has pointed out that these differences are so small that they account for only 1–5 percent of the variance in scores (Jacklin, 1979). Without going into detailed statistical theory, what this means is that, if you wanted to predict whether someone would score high or low on a spatial abilities test, knowing their sex would give you only between 1 and 5 percent of the information you would need in order to make a correct prediction. In other words, sex may sometimes play a role in one's score, but that role is tiny.

In regard to #3, the unreliability of sex differences, it is important to be aware that the differences appear more common than they are because data that show no-difference findings are often ignored. In fact, many no-difference studies are never accepted for publication, simply *because* they show no differences. But even when a no-difference result is published, it may be ignored. As Wittig (1979) has pointed out, it is commonly noted that Baughman and Dahlstrom (1968) found a male superiority in the spatial relations subtest of Thurstone's Primary Mental Abilities Test (Thurstone, 1963). However, that finding applied to a group of 437 White children. The finding that there were no sex differences for the 642 Black children in the same study is not commonly cited. This is a striking example of the way that sexism and racism can combine to result in the suppression—and eventual invisibility—of important information. A further example of the invisibility of crucial information is Parlee and Rajagopal's (1974) observation that one study often cited as evidence of a male spatial superiority (Dawson, 1967a, 1967b) in fact employed only male participants!

In regard to point #4, since those sex differences that do appear are not usually found until adolescence, it is extremely doubtful that innate factors are involved.

## ❖ BUILDING THEORIES ON SHIFTING SANDS

Based on the kind of flimsy evidence just described, theories have been created to "explain" the "sex difference" in "spatial abilities." It is irresponsible and damaging to create a theory that has little or no foundation in data, because once a theory exists, both scholars and laypeople tend to assume that the theory is based on solid evidence. Then, rarely does anyone check to see whether there are data that justify the theory. Interestingly, the theorists have tended to claim that these so-called sex differences are innate, inevitable, unchangeable.

Let us look at two theories and their major flaws, which show that, even if they had been based on solid evidence, the theories themselves don't hold water.

**1. Genetic Theory.** According to the major genetic theory about sex differences in spatial abilities, these abilities are sex-linked through the X chromosome. The theory is somewhat complicated, but if it were true, then mothers' and sons' scores on a spatial abilities test (if a legitimate spatial test could be found) should be more similar to each other than mothers' and daughters' scores, and there should be no correlation at all between fathers' and sons' scores.

In fact, however, the data do *not* fit this pattern, but an important reviewer of the literature (Harris, 1978) first presents the data and then claims that this genetic theory *is* true. He says, "the model of spatial ability as a recessive sex-linked trait can stand" (p. 449). If one didn't look at the actual numbers in the data but only at theorists' and reviewers' claims, one would assume that the genetic theory was well supported.

**2. Brain Lateralization Theories.** Many different theories about alleged sex differences in spatial abilities have been proposed. These have been based on the assumption that sex differences in the brain give rise to differences in performance on "spatial" tests. A revealing fact is that these theories conflict with each other, so they cannot all be true. Some theorists (e.g., Levy, 1970) claim that spatial abilities are superior when based in one hemisphere of the brain, whereas others (e.g., Buffery & Gray, 1972) claim that they are better when based in both hemispheres. To complicate matters even more, McGuinness (1980) has suggested that "*both* hemispheres appear to operate in all tasks" (p. 244).

Finally, as a number of scholars have pointed out (see Caplan et al., 1985, for a review), in the area of research on brain functioning, many studies are poorly done and/or are carried out on atypical populations (e.g., people whose brains are diseased or damaged), and a few studies can be found to support just about any theory.

The great variety of activities known as spatial abilities have in common the fact that they are activities at which males are considered to excel. If tests of spatial ability included the ability to judge how much flour is in a cup, or how to use a dress pattern in sewing, the results might look quite different. Spatial abilities may very well be based on stereotypically male abilities. The wonder is that in spite of this, the few differences found between females' and males' spatial abilities are small and unreliable. If scientists were to stop using the concept of spatial abilities, it would create an environment in which they could take a fresh look at individual people's varied abilities to learn and at blocks to their learning—and that would be helpful to both sexes.

# References

Annett, M. (1980). Sex differences in laterality—meaningfulness versus reliability. *The Behavioral and Brain Sciences, 3,* 227–228.

Baughman, E. E., & Dahlstrom, W. G. (1968). *Negro and white children: A psychological study in the rural south.* New York: Academic Press.

Buffery, A., & Gray, J. (1972). Sex differences in the development of spatial and linguistic skills. In C. Ounsted & D. Taylor (Eds.), *Gender differences, their ontogeny and significance* (pp. 123–158). Edinburgh: Churchill Livingstone.

Caplan, P. J., MacPherson, G. M., & Tobin, P. G. (1985). Do sex-related differences in spatial abilities exist? A multilevel critique with new data. *American Psychologist, 40*(7), 786–799.

Cooper, L. A., & Shepard, R. N. (1973). Chronometric studies of the rotation of mental images. In W. G. Chase (Ed.), *Visual information processing* (pp. 75–76). New York: Academic Press.

Dawson, J. L. M. (1967a). Cultural and physiological influences upon spatial-perceptual processes in West Africa (Part I). *International Journal of Psychology, 2,* 115–128.

Dawson, J. L. M. (1967b). Cultural and physiological influences upon spatial-perceptual processes in West Africa (Part II). *International Journal of Psychology, 2,* 171–185.

Foley, J. E., & Cohen, A. J. (1984). *Gender differences in cognitive mapping.* Paper presented at the Toronto Area Women's Research Colloquium, Toronto, Canada.

French, J. W. (1951). The description of aptitude and achievement tests in terms of rotated factors. *Psychometric Monographs* (No. 5). Chicago: University of Chicago Press.

Guilford, J. P. (1947). *Printed classification tests* (Army Air Forces Aviation Psychology Research Program Report No. 5). Washington, DC: U.S. Government Printing Office.

Harris, L. J. (1978). Sex differences in spatial ability: Possible environmental, genetic, and neurological factors. In M. Kinsbourne (Ed.), *Asymmetrical function of the brain* (pp. 405–522). New York: Cambridge University Press.

Harshman, R. A., Hampson, E., & Berenbaum, S. A. (1983). Individual differences in cognitive abilities and brain organization, Part I: Sex and handedness differences in ability. *Canadian Journal of Psychology, 37,* 144–192.

Hyde, J. S. (1981). How large are cognitive gender differences? A meta-analysis using $\Omega^2$ and $d$. *American Psychologist, 36,* 892–901.

Jacklin, C. N. (1979). Epilogue. In M. A. Wittig & A. C. Petersen (Eds.), *Sex-related differences in cognitive functioning* (pp. 357–371). New York: Academic Press.

Kimball, M. M. (1981). Women and science: A critique of biological theories. *International Journal of Women's Studies, 4,* 318–338.

Levy, J. (1970). Information processing and higher psychological functions in the disconnected hemispheres of human commissurotomy patients (Doctoral dissertation, Pasadena California Institute of Technology, 1970). *Dissertation Abstracts International, 31,* 1542B.

Lips, H., Myers, A., & Colwill, N. (1978). Sex differences in ability: Do men and women have different strengths and weaknesses? In H. Lips & N. Colwill (Eds.), *Psychology of sex differences* (pp. 145–173). Englewood Cliffs, NJ: Prentice-Hall.

Maccoby, E. E., & Jacklin, C. N. (1974). *Psychology of sex differences.* Stanford: Stanford University Press.

MacFarlane-Smith, I. (1964). *Spatial ability: Its educational and social significance.* San Diego: Knapp.

McGuinness, D. (1980). Strategies, demands, and lateralized sex differences. *Behavioral and Brain Sciences, 3,* 244.

Naditch, S. F. (1976). *Sex differences in field dependence: The role of social influence.* Paper presented at the meeting of the American Psychological Association, Washington, DC.

Parlee, M. B., & Rajagopal, J. (1974). Sex differences on the embedded-figures test: A cross-cultural comparison of college students in India and in the United States. *Perceptual Motor Skills, 39,* 1311–1314.

Sherman, J. A. (1978). *Sex-related cognitive differences: An essay on theory and evidence.* Springfield, IL: Charles C Thomas.

Thurstone, L. L. (1950). *Some primary abilities in visual thinking* (Report No. 59). Chicago: University of Chicago Psychometric Laboratory.

Thurstone, L. L. (1963). *Primary mental abilities test.* Chicago: Science Research Associates.

Wittig, M. A. (1979). Genetic influences on sex-related differences in intellectual performance: Theoretical and methodological issues. In M. A. Wittig & A. C. Petersen (Eds.), *Sex-related differences in cognitive functioning* (pp. 21–65). New York: Academic Press.

# CHAPTER FIVE

# ARE BOYS BETTER THAN GIRLS AT MATH?

**M**athematics is a science, not an art. In math, you are either *right* or *wrong*. In subjects such as English and even in chemistry or physics, an answer can be partly right, but in beginning math and much of high school math, an answer is either right or wrong; you can check your answer in math to see whether it is correct. This makes math a unique arena in which to study sex differences. For instance, girls are more likely than boys to be taught to seek adults' approval (see Caplan, 1973, for a review), and one way to win approval is to give a teacher the right answer to a question. Girls may be more upset than boys by being asked questions that have single, correct answers, rather than, say, being asked to describe a character from a novel, since for the latter you can be partly right, and it is hard to be totally wrong. If a group of students take a math test, and the boys score higher than the girls, you might conclude that the boys were simply better at math. However, it is possible that the girls were worried about giving the wrong answer, and so they were less likely to try some items. This would mean that the boys were not necessarily better at that particular math skill even if their scores were higher.

Much of what we found in Chapter 4 with regard to spatial abilities also applies to the study of mathematical abilities: Most of the research yields either small sex differences or no sex differences, and the differences that do appear don't tend to emerge until around adolescence, after girls and boys have been exposed to many years of socialization about which sex is supposed to be good or bad at which school subjects. Furthermore, the results of some studies (e.g., Decore, 1984) show that females' grades in mathematics courses are actually *higher* than those of males. Decore, for instance, found that between 1970 and 1982 at the University of Alberta, females' grades in both elementary and intermediate calculus were nearly always higher than those of males. And Hanna (1988) reports, based on her study of math ability in 18 different countries, that "gender-related differences in achievement vary considerably both within and among countries" (p. 14).

Since it is so generally believed that not only are boys and men superior at math but also that this alleged difference is *innate*, it is important to look at a number of socialization factors—at least within North America—that would tend to enhance male students' math performance and interfere with that of female students. Eccles and Jacobs (1987) found that their research indicated that junior and senior high school students' grades and the likelihood that they would even enroll in math courses are more influenced by social and attitudinal factors than by their actual ability to do mathematics. One of the best-known of these factors is math anxiety, which has been shown to be higher in girls than in boys (Eccles & Jacobs, 1987). It is interesting that students' math anxiety does not seem to be based very much on how well they have done in math in the past. In other words, girls have greater anxieties about their math ability, but this is not because their ability is inferior. Math anxiety *is* related to the grades students get in math courses and their plans to take more math courses in the future. Other social and attitudinal factors include parents' belief that math is harder for girls than for boys (Eccles & Jacobs, 1987); the tendency for fathers to help their children with math homework more than mothers do (Meece, Parsons, Kaczala, Goff, & Futterman, 1982); the greater preponderance of men than women as teachers of advanced math courses (Meece et al., 1982); the stereotyping of math textbook materials and math games as more appropriate for boys than for girls; teachers' higher expectations for boys than for girls in terms of math performance (Meece et al., 1982); and teachers' tendency to spend more time instructing and interacting with boys than with girls in math courses (Meece et al., 1982). The production in 1992 of talking Barbie dolls that complained about math being difficult was a recent, glaring example of the persistence of such stereotyping.

Probably the most influential work on sex differences in math has been done by Benbow and Stanley (1980, 1983), and it illustrates some of the most common kinds of methodological problems in research on sex differences in math, so we shall examine one of their most important studies in some detail. One major reason for its importance is that it was widely publicized in the media. Some of the typical headlines (cited by Eccles & Jacobs, 1987) were:

Are Boys Better at Math?
(*New York Times*, December 7, 1980)
Do Males Have a Math Gene?
(*Newsweek*, December 15, 1980)
The Gender Factor in Math. A New Study Says Males May Be Naturally Abler Than Females
(*Time*, December 15, 1980)

Clearly, the media took the Benbow and Stanley research very seriously. Those headlines strongly suggest that boys are actually better at math than girls. Furthermore, people have believed for a long time that males are superior to females in mathematical ability, so the interpretation of Benbow and Stanley's results agreed with the accepted outlook. If we look deeper, however, we find that the reality of their work doesn't match the headlines. Moreover, the flaws in Benbow and Stanley's research are typical of the majority of sex-difference studies of math.

Benbow and Stanley (1980, 1983) studied the scores that Grade 7 and Grade 8 gifted students achieved on the mathematics portion of the Scholastic Aptitude Test (SAT-M), a test widely used to help determine who is admitted to college. Students scoring in at least the top 2–5 percent of any standardized math achievement test were invited to take the SAT. They came mainly from the Middle Atlantic area, although later on, some students from elsewhere in the United States were included. Nearly 50,000 students accepted the invitation. Benbow and Stanley found that, overall, the boys achieved higher scores than the girls. They therefore concluded that boys have greater "math reasoning ability."

There are several major errors in that research. Some of these are embedded in the design of the study, while others are just wrong interpretations of the results. Each will be discussed in detail, but briefly, they are:

1. **Measuring Math Reasoning Ability.** The researchers used the SAT-M as an indicator of "math reasoning ability," even though this test is not an accurate indicator of math aptitude.

2. **Obtaining a Uniform Sample.** We can only reasonably conclude that a difference exists between the sexes if the groups are identical in all other ways. The researchers stated that the boys and girls in the study had equal amounts of formal education. This may be true, but even when the subjects spend the same number of hours in the classroom, many factors are involved in learning other than simply the quantity of time spent in the classroom. For instance, having heard that "girls aren't very good at math" or "girls who are good at math aren't very feminine" could have important effects on students of both sexes. Futhermore, in keeping with traditional female socialization, more intelligent girls than boys may have had too little self-confidence to accept the invitation to take the SAT and participate in the research.

3. **The Power of Suggestion.** The researchers did not consider the fact that the students' expectations about their own performance, as well as other people's expectations of them, might have affected their performance on the SAT-M.

4. **From Specific to General.** The researchers wrote as though the results from their study would apply to all females and males, everywhere. This is not a valid assumption.

5. **The Unjustified Claim That Males' Superiority Is Innate.** Nowhere do they cite conclusive evidence of this.

## ❖ MEASURING "MATH REASONING ABILITY"

Benbow and Stanley wanted to compare the "mathematical reasoning ability" of boys and girls. They neglected, however, to define the phrase, so we don't know what they intended to study. How can we know whether or not the SAT-M accurately measures what they call "mathematical reasoning ability"? Since the acronym, SAT, stands for Scholastic Aptitude Test, perhaps we were meant to assume that Benbow and Stanley felt they were measuring aptitude. However, scores on the SAT-M are influenced by many factors other than pure aptitude. If you ask a person to solve a problem, but the problem requires the person to know the quadratic formula, it is impossible to solve the question without that knowledge. Then, does the question measure aptitude or achievement? It means nothing about the person's ability to solve the problem if they don't know the formula.

One possible use of a test of mathematical ability might be to predict how well a student would do in college math courses; however, the test Benbow and Stanley studied is not very useful in making such predictions. Slack and Porter (1980) found in their research that high school math grades, and even math achievement test scores, were more reliable than SAT-M scores for predicting a student's math achievement in college. Furthermore, Fox and Cohn studied students in junior high school and found that the girls' SAT-M scores were unreliable predictors of their achievement later in school.

Fox, Tobin, and Brody (see Kolata, 1980) interviewed many of the girls in the Benbow and Stanley study and found that a great many of them did not want to participate in accelerated math classes. They were afraid that their peers would think of them as "different," and they thought that the accelerated classes were dull and that the boys in the classes were "little creeps." Although the researchers did not interview the boys in the same way, their results suggest that girls believe it is not socially acceptable or desirable for them to do well in math; this belief could certainly hinder their math performance, especially since girls are more likely than boys to seek social acceptance (Caplan, 1973).

## ❖ THE PROBLEM OF OBTAINING A UNIFORM SAMPLE

Benbow and Stanley called what they found a "sex difference" in math. If the girls and boys they tested were identical in every way except for their sex, it would be fairly safe to assume that something about maleness and femaleness led to the difference in math scores. But it is *not* legitimate to make that assumption if the girls and boys differ in some way besides their sex. One of Benbow and Stanley's major assumptions was that all of their students had the same amount of formal education. Their reason for believing this was that every student was in Grade 7 in a U.S. school. However, the issue of the quantity of educational experience is much more complex. Grade 7 girls and boys don't necessarily receive the same amount of formal education, even when they are in the same classes (Eccles & Jacobs, 1987). Leinhardt, Seewald, and Engel (1979) found that by Grade 7, math teachers have spent up to 36 more hours instructing boys than girls. With less exposure to math, it is easy to see how girls might have less desire to study math.

Aside from simply the number of hours spent with each student, there is also the factor of how the teacher treats the child. Stanley himself (reported by Holden, 1987) noticed that females are more oriented toward social interaction and aesthetics, while males tend to be more oriented toward the quantitative, abstract, "power and control" (p. 661). If he is right about this, then maybe math teachers tend to teach in a style that appeals more to males than to females. This could easily explain the discrepancy in females' and males' scores. In fact, Patricia Casserly (reported by Kolata, 1980) studied 20 schools in which the members of both sexes scored equally on the math achievement tests and found they had several common features; for instance, the math teachers of these students communicated a love of and enthusiasm for math. This may have enhanced their interpersonal connections with students—a factor that the girls might have found particularly encouraging (Gilligan, 1982).

People don't learn from formal education alone; therefore girls' and boys' SAT-M scores might have been affected differentially by experiences outside the classroom. Someone who plays math-related games will be expected to learn a lot more about math than someone who doesn't. It has been shown that boys are more likely to be involved in mathematical games and math-related activities, and to read more math-related books than are girls (Astin, 1974; Fox & Cohn, 1980; Leinhardt, Seewald, & Engel, 1979).

In several ways other than biological sex, then, the girls and boys in the Benbow and Stanley study may well have differed from each other, and those other ways could certainly have led to a sex difference in the sexes' average math scores. This raises the possibility that boys may not be innately better than girls at math—as the headlines have implied—but simply have more experience with math.

## ❖ THE POWER OF SUGGESTION

In our society, boys are expected to be better at math than girls. This expectation could heavily influence the results of the SAT-M. If you lead a person to expect something, they tend to interpret whatever happens as bearing out what they were led to expect. For instance, teachers who are told that a child is not very bright tend to notice things that confirm that expectation (Rosenthal & Jacobson, 1968).

In the same way, children who are told "you cannot do math" tend to come to believe that. (Of course, usually these messages are more subtle, but just as powerful.) Then, whenever they are confronted with a mathematical problem, they are likely to conclude automatically that they cannot solve the problem and, therefore, they are less motivated to try or persist. After study-ing the various influences on students' math grades, Eccles and Jacobs (1987) concluded that the strongest influence on a student's math ability was how their mother thought they would do.

Miele (1958) found that as children get older, the difference in scores for boys and girls on the Wechsler Intelligence Scale for Children (WISC) becomes greater and greater (with boys doing better). Also, in her review of the literature on sex-difference research using the WISC, Attard (1986) con-cluded, "It appears that, on the whole, no gender differences are evident on the arithmetic sub-test [of the WISC and WAIS] up to approximately age 16" (p. 14). These results seem to reinforce the hypothesis that sex differ-ences in math result at least partly from other people's influence; as children approach age 16, they accumulate more and more years of exposure to the idea that boys are better than girls at math. Since people in our society tend to *believe* that boys are better than girls at math, it ends up appearing to be true on test results.

## ❖ FROM SPECIFIC TO GENERAL

Finally, Benbow and Stanley did not take into account what are called *sam-pling errors*. Since they studied a sample of about 50,000 Grade 7 students in the United States, even if their results were valid, they should only be assumed to apply to Grade 7 students in the United States. It is quite possible that even the results that Benbow and Stanley produced would be different for Grade 1 students or college students or 40-year-olds or 80-year-olds. It is also quite possible that the results would be different in another country, since Hanna (1988) and Schildkamp-Küngider (1982) tested tens of thousands of students from all over the world and found that in some areas, girls got the higher scores, while in other places, boys did.

Even if Benbow and Stanley's results had been otherwise accurate, they would still only apply to the specific people they tested. And it must be remembered that the people they studied were a *highly* selected group: They represent not students in general but only students who had scored in the top 2–5 percent on one of several math tests *and* who accepted the invitation to participate in the study. If, for instance, there is no sex difference in math abil-ity for 95–98 percent of students, then Benbow and Stanley's claim to have found sex differences in math is a serious distortion.

If there *were* compelling evidence that most or all boys have better math abilities than most or all girls, then it might have been reasonable to consider adjusting our education system and our way of thinking accordingly (for example, having teachers spend more time teaching girls). However, if there *is* no sex difference, or only a small, unreliable, and late-developing one or a dif-ference for only a small fraction of people, then it is dangerous to talk about "a sex difference"; to talk in that way leads people to believe that girls just can't do math. Indeed, that claim *has* been made, and many females who might have done quite well in a math career—in teaching of math; in accounting; in statistics, surveys, and poll-taking; in computer-related fields have therefore not pursued one.

As a result, for sex-difference studies about math, as for all sex-difference research, it is essential to be aware of possible sources of error, since these distort our view of the truth about females and males.

## ❖ THE UNJUSTIFIED CLAIM THAT MALES' SUPERIORITY IS INNATE

When Benbow and Stanley's work was reported at the 1986 American Association for the Advancement of Science meeting, Benbow claimed that hormonal differences lead to males' greater proficiency in math. Naturally, the media eagerly reported this story. What they did *not* mention was that hormonal levels of the students in their study were never measured, thus making Benbow's claim entirely unjustified (Caplan, 1987). This is a particularly important issue, since when there is, or seems to be, a biologically based and innate difference such as a hormonal one, people are likely to assume that little or nothing can be done to reduce the supposed inferiority of one sex.

A careful exploration of the nature of Benbow's claim about a hormonal basis for males' alleged superiority in math is useful because it reflects so many of the errors that can occur when theory and research are not thought about carefully. Although the following discussion is very detailed and complicated, it is worth going through, because it illustrates how an unfounded theory can be used as a basis for assumptions, predictions, and hypotheses. Then, data are gathered on the basis of those assumptions and hypotheses, and authors tend to try to interpret them in a way that supports the shaky theory. It is very important to remember that, *once data have been gathered to test a theory, the theory often comes to seem to be true, even if the data do not support the theory particularly well.*

In a paper titled "Extreme mathematical talent: A hormonally induced ability?" (1987), Camilla Benbow and Robert Benbow presented their "yes" answer to the question in the title of their paper. As you will see, their argument is very roundabout and complicated, and there are problems every step of the way. It is based on the unsupported theory of two other researchers.

Benbow and Benbow (1987) noted that Geschwind and Behan (1982) had reported that left-handed people are more likely than right-handers to suffer from immune disorders, learning disabilities, and migraines, and that Geschwind and Behan "hypothesized" that this was due to high levels of the "male" hormone, testosterone. Benbow and Benbow (1987) failed to mention that this claim by Geschwind and Behan has been vigorously criticized and has not actually been proven true by solid research. The Benbows suggested that testosterone slows down the development of the left hemisphere of the brain, so that the right hemisphere compensates by growing stronger, and that this improves mathematical abilities. Therefore, they concluded, excellent math students should have more immune problems and be more likely to be left-handed than would the general population. They decided to test those speculations on a group of students, but for no apparent reason they left out migraines. So, they were investigating the *implications* of only *part* of a theory, and the theory itself was not well supported in the first place. Furthermore, as we shall see, the students they studied were a highly unusual group.

The Geschwind and Behan theory was based partly on the idea that the immune disorders result from the effects of testosterone on the immune system's thymus gland. However, Benbow and Benbow (1987) cite no evidence for this idea. The theory was also based partly on the idea that testosterone slows down the development of the brain's left hemisphere, so that the right hemisphere compensates by growing stronger. However, Benbow and Benbow (1987) cite no evidence for this idea either.

What about the Benbows' speculation that mathematical tasks are better carried out by the right than the left hemisphere of the brain? They cite no evidence for this claim but simply assert that this is "considered to be" the case. In fact, however, many aspects of math involve the ability to think analytically, which in most people is located in the left hemisphere, and other aspects of math involve the ability to deal with spatial relationships of the kind that in most people are housed in the right hemisphere. Thus, it is just too simplistic to say that math tasks should be better performed when the right hemisphere is doing them.

Even *if* all of the claims and speculations by both pairs of authors had been proven to be true, then one would expect *most* males to be far better at math and much more likely to develop immune disorders and migraines and to be left-handed than most females. But that is certainly not the case.

Based on all of these unproven propositions, the Benbows *speculated* that, since males tend to have more testosterone than females, *some* males would be both left-handed and skilled at math, due to the hormone's effect on the right hemisphere, and that same testosterone would affect their thymus gland, so that they would have immune disorders. Next, they predicted that, in their very special, unusual group—the most extremely skilled math students (they had scored 700 or more on the college entrance SAT-M *before age 13* and were 1 in 10,000 students!)—left-handedness and high mathematical *reasoning* ability would be correlated with each other. They did not explain why they chose to look at math reasoning rather than at any other math abilities, and nowhere in their paper did they present any evidence that math reasoning is more likely to be affected by testosterone or by hand preference or by the brain hemispheres than any other math ability.

The Benbows claimed that they had supported their hypothesis when they found that, in their highly unusual group, there were about twice as many left-handers and twice the frequency of allergies (an immune disorder) as in the general population. However, as every introductory psychology student learns, left-handers are more common in a wide range of unusual populations, including prisoners and students at Harvard University. Therefore, it is extremely difficult to know how to interpret yet another example of a high incidence of left-handers in an extreme population. And as for the unusually high frequency of allergies in the top math students, so little is understood about allergies themselves and about possible effects of hormones on allergies that it is premature to make too much of that finding. Furthermore, a carefully done study would include investigation of the whole spectrum of immune disorders, when we have been given no reason to believe that only one specific type would be affected by testosterone levels.

Then we might wonder how the Benbows might explain why only *some* members of their highly selected group fit the pattern that their questionable theory predicted. In fact, they again plunge into speculation, suggesting that *those* students *might have been* exposed before birth to higher than normal testosterone levels. Do they present any data to support this claim? Their argument here becomes quite strange and again convoluted. They had no proof that these students had had such prenatal exposure, but they hauled out the finding that they were more likely than most students to have been born during months that have more than 12 hours of daylight per day. Then, they stated, "Daylight affects pineal gland secretion, altering the level of melatonin, which in turn has an inhibitory effect on reproductive hormones" (pp. 150–151). In other words, daylight affects Factor A, which affects Factor B, and *that* can reduce the hormone level. Aside from the sheer length of this unproven explanation about how top math students *might* have been exposed to high levels of testosterone, their reasoning is simply wrong. If more daylight is supposed to *reduce* the reproductive hormones, then these students should have had *less* testosterone, not more, than most students. And according to the Benbows' own (unsupported) chain of reasoning, lower testosterone levels should lead to *poorer* mathematical abilities.

If you look back at the headlines cited earlier in this chapter, it may seem surprising that the public could be presented such claims when they are based on highly speculative theories, research on extreme groups of people, and just plain poor reasoning. However, such presentations are not uncommon. When some journalists hear what seems to be a "hot" story, they do not stop to learn whether or not there is any scientific basis for it.

We hope that, through the scrutiny of the range and variety of problems in the Benbow and Stanley study, you have some sense of the complexity and difficulty of the field of sex differences in mathematics. This sense should be helpful to you as you read other research or plan your own.

## References

Astin, H. (1974). Sex differences in mathematical and scientific precocity. In J. Stanley, D. Keating, & L. Fox (Eds.), *Mathematical talent: Discovery, descriptions, and development* (pp. 70–86). Baltimore, MD: Johns Hopkins University Press.

Attard, M. (1986). *Gender differences on the Arithmetic and Coding subtests of the Wechsler Intelligence Scale for Children.* Unpublished master's thesis, University of Toronto.

Benbow, C. P., & Benbow, R. M. (1987). Extreme mathematical talent: A hormonally induced ability? In David Ottoson (Ed.), *Duality and unity of the brain* (pp. 147–157). London: Macmillan.

Benbow, C., & Stanley, J. (1980, December 12). Sex differences in mathematical ability: Fact or artifact? *Science, 210,* 1262–1264.

Benbow, C., & Stanley, J. (1983, December 2). Sex differences in mathematical reasoning: More facts. *Science, 222,* 1029–1031.

Caplan, P. J. (1987, February). *Do sex differences in spatial abilities exist?* Presented at the Symposium on Bias in Sex-Differences Research, American Association for the Advancement of Science, Annual Meeting, Chicago.

Caplan, P. J. (1973). *Sex differences in determinants of antisocial behavior.* Unpublished doctoral dissertation, Duke University.

Decore, A. M. (1984). Vive la différence: A comparison of male-female academic performance. *Canadian Journal of Higher Education, 14*(3), 34–58.

Eccles, J. S., & Jacobs, J. E. (1987). Social forces shape math attitudes and performance. In M. R. Walsh (Ed.), *The psychology of women: Ongoing debates* (pp. 341–354). New Haven: Yale University Press.

Fox, L., & Cohn, S. (1980). Sex differences in the development of precocious mathematical talent. In L. Fox, L. A. Brody, & D. Tobin (Eds.), *Women and the mathematical mystique* (pp. 94–112). Baltimore: Johns Hopkins University Press.

Geschwind, N., & Behan, P. (1982). Left-handedness: Association with immune disease, migraine, and developmental learning disorder. *Proceedings of the National Academy of Sciences, 79,* 5097–5100.

Gilligan, C. (1982). *In a different voice: Psychological theory and women's development.* Cambridge, MA: Harvard University Press.

Hanna, G. (1988). Mathematics achievement of boys and girls: An international perspective. In D. Ellis (Ed.), *Math 4 girls* (pp. 14–21). Ontario Educational Research Council.

Holden, C. (1987, May 8). Female math anxiety on the wane. *Science, 236,* 660–661.

Kolata, G. B. (1980, December 12). Math and sex: Are girls born with less ability? *Science, 210,* 1234–1235.

Leinhardt, G.; Seewald, A.; & Engel, M. (1979). Learning what's taught: Sex differences in instruction. *Journal of Educational Psychology, 71*(3), 432–439.

Meece, J. L.; Parsons, J. E.; Kaczala, C. M.; Goff, S. B.; & Futterman, R. (1982). Sex differences in math achievement: Toward a model of academic choice. *Psychological Bulletin, 91,* 324–48.

Miele, J. A. (1958). Sex differences in intelligence: The relationship of sex to intelligence as measured by the Wechsler Adult Intelligence Scale and the Wechsler Intelligence Scale for Children. *Dissertation Abstracts International, 18,* 2213.

Rosenthal, R., & Jacobson, L. (1968). *Pygmalion in the classroom: Teacher expectation and pupils' intellectual development.* New York: Holt, Rinehart & Winston.

Schildkamp-Küngider E. (Ed.) (1982). *International review on gender and mathematics.* ERIC Clearinghouse for Science, Mathematics, and Environmental Education, Columbus, OH.

Slack, W., & Porter, D. (1980). Training, validity, and the issue of aptitude: A reply to Jackson. *Harvard Educational Review, 50*(3), 392–401.

# CHAPTER SIX

# THE MYTH OF WOMEN'S MASOCHISM

We often hear people say—usually about a woman—"She brings her problems on herself" or "She really loves to suffer." Sometimes, they even say, "I think she's a masochist." (The term *masochist* refers to a person who actually enjoys suffering.)

Decades ago, the psychoanalyst Sigmund Freud and his colleagues actually claimed that one of the basic "feminine" traits is masochism. In fact, Freud's disciple Helene Deutsch (1944) asserted that the three fundamental "feminine" traits, common to all girls and women, were masochism, passivity, and narcissism. Freud and his colleagues said that *all* women are masochists. Since the enjoyment of suffering seems bizarre and deeply disturbed, the implication was that "normal" women, all women, were psychologically disturbed. This is a belief that persists even today. Many psychotherapists—and laypeople—still believe that all women or many women are masochistic, and even at parties one hears comments like the ones quoted above. Occasionally, such remarks are made about men, but they are not nearly as common.

Many people who believe that women enjoy suffering use that belief as an excuse for not doing anything to improve the ways that girls and women are treated in our society. For instance, when they are told, "Millions of North American women live with men who beat them," they tend to give answers like, "Well, they must enjoy it, or they wouldn't stay." If you are satisfied with that kind of excuse, then you don't have to look at the *real* reasons for women's problems. So, for example, in the case of battered wives, you don't have to consider that many battered women stay with the men who beat them because:

> they have learned that a good woman always stands by her man, and if he is violent, it is her responsibility to tame him;

they know that since women's salaries are only two-thirds as high as men's salaries, as single mothers they would have trouble supporting themselves and their children; or

they are afraid of being alone, and they think that if they leave this man, no one else will want them (this belief is often created or intensified by the experience of the abuse itself).

There are other reasons, too, that battered women stay with the men who beat them, but the main point is that *they do NOT stay because they enjoy the suffering.* And, assuming that women are masochistic prevents us from exploring and understanding the real reasons they stay, so that we could do something to help them. The same kinds of principles apply to women who are unhappy for various reasons. For instance, a woman who is underpaid but stays in her job may do so because high-paying jobs are hard for women to get, because she likes her boss and co-workers, or a host of other reasons—*not* because she enjoys being underpaid.

Many people, especially women, who have gone to therapists because they were feeling unhappy (for various reasons) and wanted to feel better have described the following sequence of events: They would tell the therapist that they were feeling terrible because their male partner was beating them or was cold to them, because they were being sexually harassed or denied promotions they deserved at work, because they were overwhelmed by the tasks of motherhood, and so on. During each visit, the therapist would listen to their descriptions of the upsetting events of the previous week and then make a comment such as, "Do you see how you bring your misery on yourself?"—blaming the patient for her own unhappiness. If the patient ever ventured to say, "But I *don't* try to make these things happen, and I don't enjoy them!" it was not uncommon for the therapist to reply, "Not consciously, you don't, but that just means that your self-harming motives are *un*conscious."

What these patients learned, then, from such therapists was to feel helpless and hopeless about their lives. Many have reported that, believing their problems to come from their sick, masochistic unconscious processes, they gave up trying to make their lives better. As one woman said:

> If I leave Fred, who hits me every payday when he gets drunk, then what I've learned from my therapist is that, even if I *tried* to choose a nice, gentle man the next time, my sick unconscious would drive me right toward the most abusive man in the room. Even if he didn't seem to be abusive, I apparently could sense his potential to be violent, and my unconscious would propel me toward him. So I might as well stick with what I've got.

Most of the professionals who have supported the theory of women's masochism have been psychotherapists who have not made any attempt to do systematic research on the women they call masochists; they have simply made their claim and then acted as though it were true. You may find it surprising that very little research has been done on such an important subject, that such an unfounded claim can be accepted as truth, but that is the case. By 1989, only five articles (two of them not published) could be located through a combined computer and manual search of relevant materials in which there was any report of any attempt to do systematic research on women and masochism; even those studies were poorly done (Caplan & Gans, 1989). Only one of these studies—done by Robert May—is about women and masochism in a general way; the other four (Kass, MacKinnon, & Spitzer, 1986; Kass, Spitzer, Williams, & Widiger, n.d.; Reich, 1987; Spitzer, Williams, Kass, & Davies, n.d.) are reports of technical studies designed to see *if there should be* a category of emotional disturbance for "masochistic personalities." (For a detailed critique of one of these studies—Kass, MacKinnon, & Spitzer, 1986—see Caplan, 1987.) It is indeed astonishing that an entire category of emotional disturbance could be proposed and *four* specialized studies of that category could be produced, when only *one* scientific, empirical study has been done to try to prove that this phenomenon even exists. It is instructive to realize that this can happen, because this is one way in which females have been made to seem more emotionally disturbed than males.

The topic of women and masochism has given rise to a great many theoretical papers and many case studies, which are a therapist's description of one or two patients (in this case, patients the therapist regards as masochistic). But in case studies and theoretical articles it is especially easy for authors' biases to affect what they write, because without large amounts of evidence to contradict an author's pet theory or point of view, there is little to counterbalance personal prejudices.

Let us look carefully at Robert May's study. It is an important study because, even though it was published in 1966, it illustrates both a type of thinking still very common among therapists and a number of problems that continue to plague current research on masochism as well as on a host of other topics related to sex and gender studies.

## ❖ MAY'S STUDY

In 1966, Robert May's paper called "Sex Differences in Fantasy Patterns" was published. May writes that the purpose of the study is to demonstrate that males and females have different fantasy patterns, and he labels the female one "masochistic." May's article illustrates many important points that are relevant both to the work on women's alleged "masochism" and to scientific research in general:

1. Research can be presented as though it *proves* that a theory is correct, even though it does not.

2. Researchers can design a study to try to gather proof of a theory without first thinking or writing logically about whether that theory makes sense *or* is supported by any strong evidence.

3. Researchers can use instruments that are only slightly related to what they claim they are studying—but even so can claim that the information gathered by using these instruments does relate to the topic.

4. Researchers can describe, summarize, or interpret data in inaccurate or misleading ways.

## ■ May's Approach and Theory

Now we shall look in detail at May's article. May does not examine thoughtfully or make any attempt to criticize the claims and the "evidence" about masochism in women that had been put forward before he began his own work; for example, he says that when a father throws a baby girl into the air, and she looks frightened but also laughs, that proves she enjoys the suffering. What he does *not* say is that she might have *mixed* feelings about the experience (as do many adults of both sexes about roller coaster rides, for instance); she might feel scared about the height and the fear that she might be dropped but feel jubilant and amused each time she is caught and realizes that what she feared would happen did not come true. Nor does May address the fact that many male babies look frightened but also laugh when thrown in the air or that, if anything that involves pain or fear deserves to be called masochistic, that label should be applied to much of what is generally considered typically male behavior (Newman & Caplan, 1982)—such as football, boxing, and wrestling—but which is usually called something admiring and appreciative, such as strong, tough, or gutsy.

Another example May offers of females' "masochism" is the fact that childbirth is painful, and only women give birth. This is a very strange claim, for many reasons, including the fact that childbirth is not painful for every mother, that not all women give birth, that women do not always become pregnant intentionally, and that even those who do become pregnant intentionally do so not because they look forward to the pain of labor and delivery but because they want to have a baby and care for a child. Men and boys, of course, experience a great deal of pain in their lives, too, but May does not suggest that the fact that males experience some pain means that *they* enjoy it; this kind of "reasoning" is reserved only for thinking about females' motives and fantasies. Also, women *endure* the pain because they know, or hope, the result will be worth it. Male bodybuilders do the same.

Thus, May bases his own research on a theory for which he does not even provide convincing evidence (indeed, Caplan, 1987, argues that there *is* no convincing evidence for the theory that women enjoy suffering).

When May tries to describe masochism, he says that "feminine masochism could be defined as a typical *sequence* or pattern of action and feeling. Suffering following [sic] by joy, failure followed by success, risking oneself followed by love" (p. 302). This is very different from the usual definition of masochism, which involves not pleasure *after* pain but enjoyment of pain *itself.* However, May does not even try to justify his change to a new definition. Furthermore, he takes no notice of the fact that, for men as well as for women, joy often follows suffering, success follows failure, and love follows risk—and yet his entire paper is based on his aim of gathering evidence that women's fantasy patterns are masochistic and that men's are of a quite different type.

May says that the "male pattern" of fantasy is the reverse of the "feminine masochistic" one, that the male pattern involves a good experience or achievement followed by a decline or failure.

### ■ May's Method

To test his hypothesis that females and males have different fantasy patterns, May chose a *projective* method, in which people were shown pictures and asked to make up stories about them. Clinicians who use such techniques generally believe that people "project" or consciously or unconsciously use their own life experiences, attitudes, feelings, and fantasies in making up their stories. (There is a long-standing debate about the extent to which projective tests really work in that way.)

May had 60 female and 44 male college students write stories in response to four pictures he chose. He then had scorers classify each story for patterns of "deprivation followed by enhancement" (what he considered the "feminine" pattern) or the reverse ("enhancement followed by deprivation," what he considered the "masculine" pattern). The pictures, according to May, "were selected with the aim of including a broad, yet pertinent, range of people and situations" (p. 303)—that is May's claim, but he apparently made no attempt to find out whether these pictures were pertinent to his hypothesis or whether they actually represented a broad range. In fact, he used only four pictures, a very small number for such an important study. Furthermore, there are problems with at least two of the four.

Picture A showed a man and woman doing a midair trapeze act; Picture B, a young bullfighter walking in the ring; Picture C, a shabby man and barefoot woman sitting on a stone bench; and Picture D, a child of unclear sex leaping or running in a field with a bird flying above. Although it makes sense that Picture A might tend to encourage stories that involve rising and falling, trapeze artists are very sex-role-stereotyped, with the strong male catching the lighter female flying through the air. The problem with that is that strongly stereotypic pictures are likely to elicit stories that are heavily determined by *socialization* experiences (what people learn from society and family), but May's theory is that women's "masochistic" fantasies and men's "appropriate" ones are *biologically* based (develop because of genetic or inborn differences); stories told in response to this picture may not reflect *anything* about biologically based fantasies; for instance, in response to the trapeze picture, women might well write stories about fears of falling or being hurt and hopes of being caught or rescued, putting themselves in the place of the woman in the picture, who is in danger of being dropped; men, in contrast, might put themselves in the place of the male acrobat and write about how strong and powerful they feel. As the researcher scoring these stories, then, May would score the former stories as proof of women's natural masochism.

Picture B is intensely male-stereotypic, even "macho," and so it is hard to know how to interpret women's stories about it: Do their stories really reflect their own, deep fantasy patterns or just their observations of male bullfighters?

### ■ May's Results

May claims that the people he had do the scoring of the students' stories had high interrater reliability, that is, that they usually agreed about the way to score each of the students' stories. However, the first step was to have the raters decide which stories were even *scorable* according to May's system, which could be identified as revealing either a "feminine" or a "masculine" fantasy pattern. It turned out that for the stories students told about Picture D, the scorers only agreed 65 percent of the time about whether or not each story was scorable—and that was the *highest* percentage for any of the pictures. The lowest was only 32 percent (for Picture C). For all four combined, the scorers only agreed about the scorability of about half of the stories. This is an extremely low figure.

May was undeterred by this outcome. Even though the raters he had trained only agreed that about half of the stories could be scored for May's so-called "feminine and masculine" fantasy pattern, May had them go ahead and score the remaining stories, using his system. So, when we look at the results of May's study, we need to remember that at least half of the stories did not even fit May's theory well enough to be given any score at all.

For the remaining scorable stories, on Picture C the scorers agreed less than half of the time about whether a story should be scored as a "feminine" or a "masculine" fantasy, and at best on the other cards they disagreed more than one-fifth of the time. So, the proportion of total stories that the scorers categorized in the same way as each other was actually *far less than one-half.*

Even when the scorers did agree, they often failed to find that females' stories followed the "masochistic" pattern and that men's did not. On Picture D (child in a field), there was *no* sex difference in scored fantasy patterns; on Picture C (man and woman on bench) *both women and men* told more "feminine-masochistic" than "masculine" stories; on Picture B (the bullfighter) the males told a fair number of "masculine" stories, but the females apparently told no more "feminine-masochistic" than "masculine" ones; and *only* on Picture A (the trapeze artists) did the females apparently tell more "feminine-masochistic" and the males, more "masculine" ones.

To summarize the results, May actually found his predicted pattern for fewer than one-half of the stories that were told in response to only *one* of the *four* pictures he used.

## ■ May's Interpretation of His Results

Although his results fall far short of his prediction, and therefore his theory that women's fantasy patterns are masochistic and men's are not was *not* supported, May then writes as though he *did* prove his theory. He even goes on to discuss the implications of this unproven pattern as though they actually existed, distracting readers' attention from the lack of proof that females are masochistic, as they become absorbed in considering the "implications" of this (unproven) theory.

## ❖ A NEW LOOK AT FEMALES AND MASOCHISM

May's article and his approach represent an old, sexist way of thinking about whether or not girls and women enjoy suffering, but both are typical of contemporary thinking as well. In fact, the powerfully influential handbook of psychiatry published by the American Psychiatric Association (*Diagnostic and Statistical Manual of Mental Disorder [3rd ed., rev.]*: APA, 1987) includes a category that is akin to the masochism belief, "Self-defeating Personality Disorder." (For critical reviews, see Caplan, 1987, and Caplan & Gans, 1991.)

As this book was going to press, we received word that a committee that was revising the handbook had just voted to take "Self-defeating Personality Disorder" out of the next edition. Although this was a positive step, it is crucial to note that the committee had not voted to remove the category during the first seven years after it was first proposed for inclusion in their book. During those years, letters and petitions from groups and individuals representing more than six million people objecting to the category had been sent to the committee. Scholars had painstakingly criticized the handful of relevant studies, showing that there was no research to prove that such a category should even exist and pointing out the dangers that it would pose for many patients, especially women (e.g. Herman, 1988; Walker, 1987; Caplan & Gans, 1991). The committee's vote to remove the category came more than a year after it had received the last of those papers but just when the category was receiving extensive, negative publicity. A psychiatrist named Dr. Margaret Jensvold was suing the National Institute of Mental Health (NIMH) because some of the male psychiatrists there had subjected her to sexual harassment and gender discrimination. Part of the NIMH's defense in the lawsuit was to be that she had "Self-defeating Personality Disorder" and thus brought her problems on herself. When a major television station and a major newspaper planned to do series on sexism in the NIMH, and the *Journal of the American Medical Association* planned to send a reporter to cover the court proceedings, the handbook's committee voted to remove the category.

As we pointed out at the beginning of this chapter, as long as we assume that females enjoy suffering, we are unlikely to look at the real causes of that suffering and to begin to do something to eliminate those causes and provide real help for suffering girls and women. Feminist theorist Nikki Gerrard (1991) has called masochism a *terminal* word, a word that causes us to believe we have found the answer, and therefore stop questioning and trying to understand what is really going on. Unfortunately, many psychotherapists to whom battered or depressed women turn for help actually believe that suffering women enjoy the pain and bring it on themselves. When they label these women "masochists," they believe that masochism is the answer to the question, "Why are these women suffering?" In this kind of therapy, then, both the therapist and the unhappy woman spend a great deal of time talking about the ways the woman is suffering, ending many sessions by concluding that they have just discussed yet another example of how she brought the suffering on herself. As Gerrard suggests, we need to stop using terminal words like "masochism," so that we clear the way to look at the true causes of women's unhappiness (such as being married to violent men, having jobs in which they are underpaid or harassed, having been raped or sexually abused, having little self-esteem because they feel that women are inferior, etc.). This is the way of the future, the path toward looking at the realities of the lives of girls and women *without* assuming that they are psychologically disturbed and that there is no point in trying to help them.

# References

Caplan, P. J. (1987). *The myth of women's masochism.* New York: Signet.

Caplan, P. J., & Gans, M. (1989). *Analysis of the empirical basis for "Self-Defeating Personality Disorder."* Prepared for SDPD subcommittee of DSM-IV Task Force.

Caplan, P. J., & Gans, M. (1991). Is there empirical justification for the category of "Self-Defeating Personality Disorder"? *Feminism and Psychology, 1,* 263–278.

Deutsch, H. (1944). *The psychology of women,* Vol. 1. New York: Grune & Stratton.

Gerrard, N. (1991). *Guilt is a terminal word: A critical and multicultural analysis of guilt in relation to mothers and daughters.* Unpublished manuscript.

Herman, J. (1988). Review of "Self-defeating Personality Disorder." Prepared for DSM-IV Work Group on Personality Disorders.

Kass, F.; MacKinnon, R. A; & Spitzer, R. L. (1986). Masochistic personality: An empirical study. *American Journal of Psychiatry, 143*(2), 216–218.

Kass, F.; Spitzer, R. L.; Williams, J. B. W.; & Widiger, T. (n.d). *Self-defeating personality disorder and DSM-III-R I: Justification for inclusion and development of the diagnostic criteria.* Unpublished manuscript.

May, R. (1966). Sex differences in fantasy patterns. *Journal of Projective Techniques, 30,* 252–259. Reprinted in J. Bardwick (Ed.), (1972), *Readings on the psychology of women* (pp. 301–307). New York: Harper & Row.

Newman, F., & Caplan, P. J. (1982). Juvenile female prostitution as gender-consistent response to early deprivation. *International Journal of Women's Studies, 5,* 128–137.

Reich, J. (1987). Prevalence of DSM-III-R self-defeating (masochistic) personality disorder in normal and outpatient population, *Journal of Nervous and Mental Disease, 175*(1), 52–54.

Spitzer, R. L.; Williams, J. B. W.; Kass, F.; & Davies, M. (n.d.) *Self-defeating personality disorder and DSM-III-R II: A national field trial of the diagnostic criteria.* Unpublished manuscript.

Walker, L. E. A. (1987). Inadequacies of the Masochistic Personality Disorder diagnosis for women. *Journal of Personality Disorders, 1,* 183–189.

# CHAPTER SEVEN

# SEX DIFFERENCES IN AGGRESSION

Men and boys are generally assumed to be more aggressive than women and girls, and this sex difference is considered to be an inborn and inevitable difference. A wide variety of social practices have been based on the assumption that males are innately more aggressive than females. These have included such disparate practices as the rule that in girls' basketball games the players could not bounce the ball more than twice, whereas in boys' basketball, the players were allowed to dribble all the way down the court; and making North American women after World War II feel that they should leave their paying jobs so that the male war veterans could have them, because women were supposedly better suited to be at home in less venturesome roles (Friedan, 1963).

As in most areas of psychological research, there has been considerable confusion about the definition of *aggression*. Some people have distinguished assertiveness from aggression and from violence, but others argue that all of these belong on a single continuum. When attempts have been made to *measure* sex differences in aggression, the kinds of behavior that have been targeted include: "Who calmly states their opinion and sticks to it?" "Who interrupts more?" "Who punches an inflated Bobo doll more?" "Who grabs more candy at the party?" "Who swears more?" "Who takes up more space?" "Who hits other people?" "Who stands up for, and protects, others?" For nearly every bit of behavior that a given author has called aggressive, other authors have said otherwise. Since some of the problems with definitional dilemmas in research are covered in more detail in Chapter 4, on Sex Differences in Spatial Abilities, they will not be covered extensively here. Keep in mind throughout this chapter that the work on sex differences in aggression, like most areas of sex-difference research, has been done against a confusing definitional backdrop. Some theorists have gone so far as to claim that human males' aggressive behavior is essential to the survival of most humans, and they "justify" this assertion by claims such as, "It's innate aggression that impels male, nonhuman animals to hunt in order to feed themselves and other members of their species," "It's innate aggression that impels male animals to protect other members of their species," and "It's innate aggression that impels male animals to fight against each other to win females so that they can get their (the males') genes into the reproductive gene pool." We shall look at these arguments about the inevitability of males' aggressiveness and then look at some of the problems that have been identified in the research that has been used as the basis of claims about males' greater aggression.

## ❖ IS MALES' GREATER AGGRESSIVENESS INNATE?[1]

It is fascinating that whatever males do has tended to be interpreted as proof of their greater aggressiveness, but the same has not been true for females' behavior. For instance, some anthropologists have pointed out that in certain cultures men hunt animals for food and women gather plants for food; then they have claimed that this is proof that males are the more aggressive sex. But why should we assume that males' hunting requires more aggressiveness than females' gathering? It is no doubt true that more *courage* is required to get close enough to a buffalo in order to spear it than to get close enough to a tuber to pull it from the ground and prepare it for dining; but is courage the same as aggression? After all, a great deal of courage is required to endure the pain that many women experience during childbirth, but that has not usually been used to prove that women are more courageous than men, and it certainly has not been equated with their aggressiveness. And even if we decide that it requires somewhat more aggressiveness to kill animals than to gather plants for food or to give birth, meat-eating is clearly not essential to the survival of the human species. Most food for most human societies has been food that is gathered and/or grown. The hunting of animals has not been proven to have been essential at any time for the survival of most humans, and therefore it is difficult to argue that contemporary males are the prisoners of innate aggressive and murderous drives because it is necessary for species survival.

Just for the moment, let us assume that males' aggression helps protect the human species from outside attackers. Even so, it *interferes with* the survival of the human species when males do not limit their aggression to hunting dangerous animals but also direct their aggression against members of their *own* species (as in wife- and child-battering, incest, and sexual assault, all of which are extremely common in the human species).

A counterargument has been proposed which goes like this:

---

1. The material in this section is covered in fascinating detail in Ruth Bleier (Ed.), *Feminist Approaches to Science.* New York: Pergamon, 1986.

Human males' aggression against members of their own species actually ensures the survival of the fittest, because men fight with each other for the right to reproduce with the best or most attractive or most robust females. This means that only the strongest humans pass on their genes.

However, this argument doesn't fit the evidence. Human males often physically attack and hurt or even kill human females and children; this, of course, explains nothing about survival of the human species and is actually dangerous to individual women, children, and the species. Human males also attack other males but not primarily in the context of vying for women. Furthermore, it has been shown that it is *not* the most aggressive individuals of the species who necessarily have the greatest reproductive "success," that is, the greatest number of offspring (Hubbard, 1990).

Finally, those theorists who have argued that males' aggression is necessary to the survival of the human species have usually used nonhuman animals' behavior to try to support their claims. However, many feminist writers have now demonstrated that traditional theorists chose very carefully the kinds of animals they studied in order to "prove" their theories. They tended to choose those kinds of animals in which males' behavior differs the most from females' behavior and those in which aggression is common rather than those in which it is relatively rare. It is now clear, however, that there are enormous variations among animal species in regard to which sex provides food and which sex provides protection as well as in the overall level of species aggression and in the size of the sex difference in aggression. Thus, if we wanted to use animals for a model to explain human behavior, we would have to choose very carefully which species to look at, and we would have to be prepared to justify our choices. Anthropologist Lila Leibowitz points out, for instance, that there is a wide variety of ways to define and measure aggression in primates and then illustrates the variability of sex differences in aggression among primate species. She writes that, among gibbons, an intruder may be driven off by either an adult male or an adult female. Furthermore, for gibbons, "in some pairs the male tends to give way to the female; in others the reverse is true" (Leibowitz, 1975, p. 25). By contrast, "the large orangutan male is rarely involved in aggressive interactions and has even less opportunity to function as a leader or protector than the male gibbon" (Leibowitz, 1975, p. 26). Among baboons, who are often used to "prove" that human males are naturally more aggressive than human females, some males

> reportedly rush to place themselves between threatening situations and the troop.... When danger threatens, males usually issue warning barks and station themselves near the threat and along an escape route.... But if danger is imminent, the first animals into the safety of the trees are those unencumbered by infants—the males. (Leibowitz, 1975, pp. 29–30)

In fact, it is hard to justify using any nonhuman animal model to prove anything about the inevitability of human behavior. Rosenberg (1973) explains the reason for this. Most theorists who claim that there are innate sex differences in human behavior try to explain these differences by saying that they are essential parts of the reproductive routine. However, as Rosenberg notes, human females are the only female animals who can be receptive to sexual intercourse regardless of menstrual cycle phase and even after menopause. Therefore, since any nonhuman female animals' behavior will differ in this extremely significant way—the implications and effects of which have not begun to be thoroughly documented—it is not truly legitimate to claim anything about humans based on other animals' sex-related behavior. Furthermore, theorists who claim that humans are far more advanced than other animals with respect to such abilities as the capacity to use language extensively and to do symbolic thinking, including certain kinds of recollections of the past and complex planning or fantasizing about the future, are often the same theorists who use those nonhuman animals' behavior to "explain" such differences as human males' allegedly greater aggression than that of human females.

The hormone testosterone, which is present in higher concentrations in most males than in most female humans and many other animals as well, is most often named as the physical basis of males' supposedly greater aggressiveness. Behind this claim is the assumption that hormones give rise to behavior, that testosterone leads to aggression. This claim is usually followed by statements about the inevitability of males' aggression, fistfights, even warfare, and so on, because of their presumably unchangeable physiological underpinnings. Although this can happen, a crucial but rarely noted fact is that the cause-effect relationship can also be the reverse: Changes in feelings and behavior can modify hormone levels. Many women are aware of this because they observe that their menstrual cycle can change as their level of activity and/or tension changes. Other examples of feelings and behavior affecting hormone levels include hormonal increases in the adrenals when a person is angry or feeling great anxiety and changes in hormones related to reproduction when a person becomes sexually aroused.

It is clear, however, that it is not simply true that hormones cause behavior; rather, hormones and behavior influence *each other*. This has been dramatically demonstrated through studies of various kinds of primates such as baboons. Although we have to keep in mind the limitations of animal studies for helping us to understand human behavior, in some cases they can be useful. For instance, in animal species that have clear and fairly stable arrangements of dominance (called *dominance hierarchies*), it is possible, through blood tests, to see whether an individual animal's position in the dominance hierarchy is correlated with the level of testosterone in its blood. In humans these dominance hierarchies are less clear and change more rapidly, making such correlations harder to monitor.

Linda Fedigan, author of the book *Primate Paradigms: Sex Roles and Social Bonds,* summarizes a great deal of research which shows that "testosterone levels are influenced by multiple environmental, social and species variables" as shown in a variety of species. One example of this is male monkeys' testosterone levels falling sharply after they have been suddenly and decisively defeated by other males (Fedigan, 1982). She continues: "The following factors have been shown to influence circulating levels of testosterone: ontogenetic status, circadian rhythms, relative access to females, seasonality, alterations in social rank, successful and unsuccessful agonistic encounters" (p. 164).

Thus, Fedigan concludes that the relationship between testosterone and aggression in nonhuman primate animals is clearly a two-way street. Perhaps even more interestingly, she reports: "Studies of the human male have generally shown no correlations between androgen ['male hormone'] levels and aggression levels" (p. 164). There are some researchers who would dispute this, but what is fascinating is that there has been a major historical shift in this area of scientific research. Whereas it used to be assumed that hormones caused behavior, that simplistic view can no longer be taken to be true.

Whether or not we assume that the animal research is relevant to human behavior, the fact that human behavior and feelings can change hormone levels has major social implications, as we shall see in the final section of this chapter.

## ❖ THE RESEARCH ON SEX DIFFERENCES IN AGGRESSION[2]

As we have seen, it is generally believed that human males are more aggressive than human females. How has that belief come about?

There has been an enormous amount of research on sex differences in human aggression. Studies that do *not* yield a sex difference have traditionally been difficult, if not impossible, to get published (Caplan, 1979). Therefore, when reviewers have looked at the *published* research in any arena related to sex differences, it has always looked as though most of the research proved the existence of a sex difference rather than little or no difference. This is now recognized to be such a problem that statisticians have designed a formula referred to as the *file drawer* statistic; that is, for every one published study showing a group difference, it is assumed (through the use of this formula) that a certain number of no-difference studies have been done that have not been published.

But, one might say, if some studies show no difference and some show that males are more aggressive, doesn't that prove that males *are* more aggressive but that it just doesn't always show up in the research? The simplest answer to that is "no." It is not legitimate or responsible to assume that the sex *difference* studies mean something and that the no-difference studies do not need to be taken into consideration. You could just as easily argue the reverse, that the sex-difference studies were faulty. What does one do about these two categories of results? One way to deal with them is to look for what is called a "boundary condition."

---

2. The material in this section is discussed in detail in Paula J. Caplan (1979), "Beyond the box score: A boundary condition for sex differences in aggression and achievement striving." In B. Maher (Ed.), *Progress in Experimental Personality Research, 9,* 1979, 41–87.

### ◼ Seeking a Boundary Condition

A *boundary condition* is a guideline that helps us to understand how studies that are supposedly of the same phenomenon—in this case, aggression—can produce very different patterns of results. Put simply, in regard to the massive research literature on sex differences in aggression, we would ask, "Is there some way in which the no-difference studies systematically differ from the studies in which males were more aggressive than females?"

This is precisely the question that formed the basis of a comprehensive review (Caplan, 1979) of the aggression literature. The focus of the review was on studies of children and adolescents, because by adulthood there has been an enormous amount of sex-differential socialization. Sex differences in adults' aggression, then, could easily be due to learned differences rather than innate ones. The same is true to a somewhat lesser extent in adolescents and children, of course; but researchers assume that children and adolescents may be less influenced by society than are adults. Since it is virtually impossible to try to study aggression in infants, one has to wait until childhood, when behavior that is clearly aggressive begins to appear. It is, however, entirely possible that even in early childhood studies, sex differences in socialization explain much, if not all, of any reported sex differences in aggression. After all, even very young boys are more likely than girls to be allowed or even encouraged to behave aggressively.

In the review of the aggression literature, a boundary condition was indeed discovered. The no-difference studies were those in which the children or adolescents believed that their behavior was unobserved. When, by contrast, they knew that they were being watched, the boys tended to be more aggressive than the girls. This supports at least two important theories—first, that sex differences in aggression are largely or entirely learned, and second, that males' greater aggression (as seen in the high incidence of men's wife-battering, sexual assault, and incest) is not inevitable *or* able to be explained away by biology. This leads us to the topic of social and political consequences of research on sex differences in aggression.

## ❖ SOME SOCIAL AND POLITICAL CONSEQUENCES OF ASSUMPTIONS ABOUT AGGRESSION

According to most traditional theories of personality, males have more powerful, less controllable aggressive and sexual drives. It is rather demeaning to men to assume that they cannot control, or take responsibility for, their urges and impulses, but the demeaning implications have usually been overlooked. Indeed, if it were really true that men were innately and unavoidably powerless to control their aggressive and sexual drives, then one would think that society would have developed ways to impose some control; for instance, men might have been forbidden to appear on the streets after dark or might have been kept out of powerful jobs where their urges might cause serious harm.

Instead, however, the claim that males' drives are innately stronger and less controllable has been used to *justify* men's imposition of their sexual and nonsexual aggression on others and to *blame* their victims—who are usually women or children—for "bringing it on themselves," allegedly by "nagging," being "seductive," or both.

More enlightened clinicians, researchers, and theorists (e.g., Caplan, 1985; Dutton & Painter, 1981; NiCarthy, 1982; Rush, 1980; Russell, 1982, 1984, 1986; L. Walker, 1979) have made it clear that men's—like women's—treatment of other people is their responsibility and it is neither accurate nor fair nor healthy to claim otherwise. Some points that should have been obvious but that were obscured by male-excusing theories have also come to light; for instance, if men really had no control over their aggressive impulses, and males were innately more aggressive than females, *all* men would inflict violence on their wives and children, and once a man started to beat his wife, he would continue until he killed her (which occasionally, but not always, happens). Recent work has shown that female and child victims do *not* bring the violence on themselves, certainly do not enjoy it, and in fact often find ingenious ways to survive and resist as much as they can in the face of terror (Caplan, 1985; NiCarthy, 1982; Russell, 1982, 1984, 1986; B. Walker, 1985; see also Chapter 6 in this volume).

In spite of this latter work, woman-blaming, girl-blaming, and man-excusing trends continue to dominate much clinical practice and theory. One example is the continuing—though no longer exclusive—claim that incest victims and their mothers, but *not* the perpetrator fathers or other men, are responsible for incest (Whitfield, 1991, has comprehensively reviewed this literature).

Another example of large-scale minimizing of adult men's responsibility for their violent acts was the American Psychiatric Association's proposal in 1985 of a category of diagnosis they called "Paraphilic Coercive Disorder." A man who had either attempted or completed a rape and who described himself as preoccupied with or compelled to rape was to be considered as having this disorder. Many associations of mental health professionals, women's groups, and laypeople protested the proposal for this category; they pointed out that it would have been easily used to convince judges to give light sentences to rapists on the grounds that their alleged "psychiatric disorder" made them not responsible for their violence, much like an insanity plea. The proposal was rejected by the association, but both before and since it was proposed, defense attorneys have frequently enlisted therapists to meet with rapists and declare that their criminal, violent behavior results from their being psychiatrically disturbed. Upon hearing these reports, judges have often said, in effect, that these men need help, not punishment, and accordingly they have imposed light jail sentences or none at all and instead ordered them to become psychotherapy patients. This has long been a common practice, *even though* psychotherapy has not been shown to stop men from committing rape.

## ❖ TOWARD A MORE ENLIGHTENED FUTURE

Some very thoughtful writers have noted that the frequency of men's aggression against their intimates is destructive to women, children, and families and the institutionalization on a huge scale of men's violence against the environment and preoccupation with warfare threaten to destroy the globe and all forms of life (Eisler, 1987; Griffin, 1978; Stoltenberg, 1989; B. Walker, 1985). Many voices are now calling for the rejection of the claim that men cannot control their violence and for an intense concentration of energy aimed at stopping men's violence in its various forms. This will require, they point out, wholesale abolition of the "macho" stereotypes, since as long as people who are described as physically male believe that they *must* behave in tough, aggressive ways, the violence will continue unabated. Pointing out that aggressors justify their aggression not only by blaming their victims but also by convincing themselves that their victims are somehow inferior, less than human, John Stoltenberg points out that to be "a real man means you get to believe that someone else is not as real" (p. 204). Stoltenberg calls men to action, urging them to take responsibility for the ways they treat others: "The core of one's being must love justice more than manhood" (p. 185).

## References

Bleier, R. (Ed.). (1986). *Feminist approaches to science.* New York: Pergamon.

Caplan, P. J. (1979). Beyond the box score: A boundary condition for sex differences in aggression and achievement striving. In B. Maher (Ed.), *Progress in experimental personality research 9*(pp. 41–87).

Caplan, P. J. (1985). *The myth of women's masochism.* New York: E. P. Dutton.

Dutton, D., & Painter, S. L. (1981). Traumatic bonding: The development of emotional attachments in battered women and other relationships of intermittent abuse. *Victimology: An International Journal, 6,* 139–155.

Eisler, R. (1987). *The chalice and the blade: Our history, our future.* San Francisco, CA: Harper & Row.

Fedigan, L. M. (1982). *Primate paradigms: Sex roles and social bonds.* Montreal: Eden Press.

Friedan, B. (1963). *The feminine mystique.* New York: Dell.

Griffin, S. (1978). *Woman and nature: The roaring inside her.* New York: Harper & Row.

Hubbard, R. (1990). *The politics of women's biology.* New Brunswick, NJ: Rutgers University Press.

Leibowitz, L. (1975). Perspectives on the evolution of sex differences. In R. Reiter (Ed.), *Toward an anthropology of women* (pp. 20–35). New York: Monthly Review Press.

NiCarthy, G. (1982). *Getting free: A handbook for women in abusive relationships.* Seattle: Seal Press.

Rosenberg, M. (1973). The biologic basis for sex role stereotypes. *Contemporary Psychoanalysis, 9*, 374–391.

Rush, F. (1980). *The best kept secret: Sexual abuse of children.* New York: Prentice-Hall.

Russell, D. E. H. (1982). *Rape in marriage.* New York: Macmillan.

Russell, D. E. H. (1984). *Sexual exploitation: Rape, child sexual abuse, and workplace harassment.* Beverly Hills: Sage.

Russell, D. E. H. (1986). *The secret trauma: Incest in the lives of girls and women.* New York: Basic Books.

Stoltenberg, J. (1989). *Refusing to be a man: Essays on sex and justice.* Portland, OR: Breitenbush Books.

Walker, B. (1985). *The crone: Woman of age, wisdom, and power.* San Francisco: Harper & Row.

Walker, L. (1979). *The battered woman.* New York: Harper & Row.

Whitfield, W. (1991). *Mother-daughter relationships in families in which fathers sexually abuse daughters.* Doctoral dissertation, Ontario Institute for Studies in Education, University of Toronto.

# CHAPTER
# EIGHT

# MOTHER-BLAME

One of the biggest mysteries that researchers and therapists have tried to solve is the question of what causes human beings' emotional problems. Experts in the field of human behavior have frequently thrown up their hands in despair because people's development is affected by *so many* factors that have direct effects and also interact with each other in complex ways to produce emotional problems.

When we want to study a fairly simple effect, that can sometimes be done; for instance, if we want to know whether factory workers become more productive when classical music is played while they work than when no music is played, we can measure their productivity with and without music. But when we want to study why a child is aggressive and destructive or why a teenager takes drugs, it is not that simple; for instance, if we suspect that treating a child in a particular way is harmful to the child, for ethical and humane reasons we cannot test it by conducting an experiment in which we decree that some children shall be treated in this possibly harmful way (Treatment A) and others shall not (Treatment B). Even if we *could* do such a thing, so many factors actually affect children that one can't guarantee that the children assigned to the different treatments are otherwise exposed to identical influences. And if they are *not* exposed to identical influences except for A and B, then we cannot be sure whether differences in those children are a result of A and B or of the other influences to which they were differentially exposed.[1]

---

1. Specialists in research methods say that if, for instance, we want to see whether treating children in a particular way (call it "Q") makes them happier than not treating them in that way, we should randomly assign each child to either the Q or the not-Q group. It is assumed that in this way, we won't accidentally end up with, say, all of the active children in the Q group and all of the calm ones in the not-Q group. If that were to happen, then we could not figure out whether the Q and not-Q children behaved diffferently because of the Q/not-Q treatment or because they were different kinds of children to begin with. However, we know that not every characteristic gets evenly distributed between groups in every study; and when the behavior we are focusing on is as complex as "mothering," the number of characteristics that could confuse the results is staggering. Even with sophisticated statistical techniques designed to help in these matters, we simply cannot be sure of controlling for all the relevant factors. In fact, we cannot even be sure that we have thought of all of the relevant factors.

That is just a small taste of the complexity involved in trying to discover how emotional problems develop. Because of this complexity and difficulty, there are huge gaps in our understanding of the causes and effects of people's unhappiness. We live in a society in which individuals—or their families—are blamed for their problems, rather than blaming harmful social factors (such as poverty, homelessness, unemployment, or racism). We tend to look for individuals and families to criticize and blame. The gap in our understanding of the causes of people's unhappiness has been filled to overflowing with researchers' and therapists' claims that mothers are to blame for their children's troubles. In this way, great quantities of time are spent in case conferences and a great deal of space is consumed in therapy journals by a myriad of ways of blaming mothers.

## ❖ IS MOTHER-BLAME EITHER JUSTIFIED OR HELPFUL?

One major problem with the pervasiveness of mother-blame is that, from a simply logical point of view, it is not justified. Even in families in which the mother is the primary caretaker, the children are exposed to a multitude of influences from other people and other sources—from the father, other relatives, family friends, teachers, peers, the media, books, and the children's own, innate characteristics (infants are known to differ from each other in temperament from birth). In a study of 125 articles written by mental health professionals for their scholarly journals, it was found that mothers were blamed for 72 different kinds of problems in their offspring, ranging from bed-wetting to schizophrenia (Caplan & Hall-McCorquodale, 1985). In that study, each article was classified according to 63 types of mother-blame, ranging from the number of words used to describe mothers and to describe fathers, to the direct attribution of children's problems to their mothers rather than their fathers, to the unquestioning acceptance of previous writers' mother-blame and incorporation of that earlier work into current explanations of children's problems. In none of the 63 categories were fathers or anyone else blamed nearly as much as mothers, and both the frequency and the intensity of mother-blame were overwhelming.

The argument that mothers *ought* to be blamed because they are the primary caretakers doesn't hold water if one looks at what the mother-blaming therapists and researchers really say. In many of the articles from the Caplan and Hall-McCorquodale study, the writers stretched ludicrously far in order to avoid blaming anyone other than the mother. For instance, one report was about a little boy called Billy, who was "school phobic"—he refused to go to school (Smith & Sharpe, 1970). Historically, school phobia has been blamed on the mother, on the theory that she is a demanding, dependent person who needs desperately to tie her child closely to her and cannot let go. In the description of Billy, this old theory is mentioned but not questioned in the least. Billy's mother is blamed for his school phobia, on the grounds that she allows him to stay home from school all day and to stay up all night watching TV. Billy's relationship with his father is described as "ideal in virtually every respect." However, it is also mentioned that Billy's father is a farmer. Where, we might ask, was Billy's father when Billy's mother was supposedly allowing Billy to stay up all night? Farmers rarely have to be out plowing the fields all night long.

Consider another example of the lengths to which writers go in order to lay the blame on mother. An author wanted to find out whether children of men who have been in prisoner-of-war camps are more likely than other children to have emotional problems (Sigal, 1976). He found that indeed this was the case. Then he wanted to understand why this was so. In studying some of these families, he observed that the former prisoners of war often felt upset and empty, and when they were in the company of their families, they weren't truly emotionally involved with them. One might have thought that the author would conclude that this explains—or helps to explain—their children's problems. However, that was not the case. The author claimed the men's problems upset their wives, and this interfered with the women's ability to provide good mothering to the children, and *that* was what caused the children's problems!

At least one of the reasons for the overwhelming tendency toward mother-blame is our society's and our mental health professionals' excessive focus on mothers: It is very simple—if you look only at mothers, you will not see other possible sources of trouble. After all, it is easier to criticize mothers than to change society. In the Caplan and Hall-McCorquodale study, it was found that even when professionals did write something about fathers, it tended to be either complimentary (as in the description of Billy's father)—something that was virtually never true of descriptions of mothers—or unrelated to emotional disturbance. One illustration of the latter comes from an article in which a child's parents are described this way: "The father, a bricklayer, was 34 yr old when the patient was born. He is healthy. The mother was 33 yr old when the patient was born; she is 'nervous'" (Nielsen et al., 1970, p. 116). In the same study, three case histories of children with a chromosomal anomaly called Klinefelter's Syndrome were reported (Nielsen et al., 1970). In these three cases, clearly the most disturbing piece of information that was given about any of the parents was that one of the fathers was emotionally abusive to his child. But when the authors drew their conclusions in trying to answer the question, "Can children with Klinefelter's Syndrome grow up psychologically normal?" their conclusion was that they could, if their *mothers* behaved properly. The abusive father's behavior seemed to have slipped through the cracks when the time came to consider the sources of trouble.

The frequency and intensity of mother-blame certainly do not seem to be justified. Furthermore, mother-blame is not only unjustified but also damaging. Whether consciously or unconsciously, most mothers realize that if anything at all goes wrong with their children, they as mothers will be held almost entirely responsible. This places mothers under intolerable pressure, pressure of a kind one rarely, if ever, encounters in paid employment. Mothers thus operate under intense strain, and this can make them anxious and fearful, so that the tasks of mothering become even more difficult than they have to be. In view of this, instead of unhesitatingly blaming mothers, it would be more appropriate to give many mothers credit for the healthy child-rearing they manage to do even though they are under so much psychological pressure, not to mention the other pressures to which many mothers are subjected because of their sex, their race, their age, their own physical or psychological hurdles, their poverty, and so on.

## ❖ WHY DOES MOTHER-BLAMING OCCUR?

If mother-blame is both so often unjustified and virtually never helpful or productive, why is it so common and so powerful? It is common not just among therapists and researchers, of course, but also among laypeople. One frequently hears people blaming their mothers for all of their problems or telling anti-mother or anti-mother-in-law jokes without anyone objecting as they might if the blame and the jokes were racist.

Mother-blame is both common and powerful because our society is still profoundly sexist (Caplan, 1989, discusses this in detail). Although the women's movement has made some people aware that it is cruel and oppressive to make demeaning comments about women in general, a resistant pocket of sexism remains in mother-blame. Many people who are aware of the damaging nature of comments that are generally sexist—such as "Women are overemotional and intrusive"—are unaware that similar comments about mothers—"Mothers are overemotional and intrusive"—also spring from wells of sexism. Since women in general are assumed to be mothers, or potential mothers, or hormonally similar to mothers, any slur against mothers is actually an implicit slur against women in general. So, in a society that continues to condone sexism in many other ways (not implementing pay equity or employment equity, not providing enough shelters or follow-up support for female victims of violence, to name just a few), it is not surprising that eradication of mother-blame has not yet begun.

Furthermore, in any society, the powerful people tend to want to keep their power. In our society, most of the economic, social, and political power is still held by men, and reinforcing mother-blame is a way to maintain the current power distribution by:

keeping mothers so insecure about their behavior that they focus intensely on being better mothers than before, rather than trying to make things easier and less oppressive for themselves and other mothers

keeping mothers so insecure about their behavior that they focus on being better mothers than other women, including their own mothers

encouraging daughters' and sons' anger at their own mothers, thus feeding the myth that mothers are incompetent, ridiculous, and so on, and keeping mothers powerless attributing major societal ills (such as juvenile delinquency, divorce, and drug abuse) to mothers, thus deflecting pressure to change away from institutions other than motherhood (such as government, the educational system, and big business)

setting women up against other women, through the methods just listed, keeping them from uniting as a source of power that could rival the powers-that-be

On a daily basis, the way that this is implemented is simple: Our society gives women the message that mothers are almost totally responsible for their children's healthy development. This drains mothers of enormous amounts of energy as they cook, clean, teach, chauffeur, and referee arguments between their children. Next, myths with which we all were raised lead us to distort our views of our mothers and mothers' view of themselves in negative ways. There are at least nine of these "Mother Myths," and they can be divided into two categories, the Perfect Mother Myths and the Bad Mother Myths (adapted from Caplan, 1989). The Perfect Mother Myths are those that set standards that are so high that no human being could possibly meet them; thus, children tend to feel their mothers don't really measure up to these ideals, and mothers themselves feel that they have failed. The Perfect Mother Myths include:

1. The measure of a good mother is a "perfect" child.

2. Mothers are endless founts of nurturance.

3. Mothers naturally know how to raise children.

4. Mothers don't get angry.

The Bad Mother Myths are those that encourage us to take our mothers' bad, neutral, or even good behavior and misinterpret it as absolutely monstrous. They include:

1. Mothers are inferior to fathers.

2. Mothers need experts' advice in order to raise healthy children.

3. Mothers are bottomless pits of emotional neediness.

4. Mothers' relationships with their teenage and adult children are sick if they are very close.

5. Mothers are dangerous when they are powerful.

(For a more detailed discussion of the ways that the various myths result in negative distortions of mothers' behavior and motives, see Caplan, 1989.)

One of the most fascinating aspects of the sets of myths is that they include some that contradict each other; for instance, a mother cannot be both endlessly giving and nurturant while being endlessly emotionally needy and demanding. Similarly, it cannot be true both that mothers naturally know everything they need to know about raising healthy children and that mothers need experts' advice in order to raise healthy children. Why do such mutually exclusive myths manage to coexist within the same society?

The answer is that they serve an important function: They are all ways to justify demeaning and mistreating mothers. Any society that wants to keep a group in a scapegoated position has to worry: "What if members of that scapegoated group do some good things? Won't that make it harder to keep laying blame on them?" Therefore, ways have to be found to take *any* good or even neutral things members of that group might do, and transform them into further proof of the group's inferiority, evil, or blameworthiness.

Since mothers are a major scapegoated group in our society, it is not surprising, then, that some mother myths contradict each other. A mother who raises a happy, healthy child is likely to receive little or no credit, because it is assumed that it took no effort or learning on her part but only "doing what comes naturally"; a mother whose child is not well-adjusted is blamed for not following experts' advice. Neither outcome is treated as evidence that some mother deserves credit or respect. Similarly, a mother who asks for *nothing* for herself receives no credit, because mothers are "naturally, inevitably, totally nurturant and giving," but a mother who does ask for a *little* something for herself is considered endlessly needy.

The myths provide the detailed directions for maintaining mother-blame, but this practice can be overcome at many levels. Anyone who cares to do so can become familiar with these myths, become sensitive to the way they affect their own thinking, just as many people have tried to become aware of their own racist, ageist, homophobic, or sexist assumptions. When we find ourselves leaping to blame mothers, or to support other people in doing so, it is important to stop and to ask whether the myths are distorting our thinking, whether there is some other way to understand the sources of a problem besides, or in addition to, looking at mothers' possible contributions.

This is important not only because it would help to alleviate a biased, damaging source of pressure that is placed on mothers but also because it would help us to understand the real causes of people's problems by blocking the mother-blaming path of least resistance.

Therapists, researchers, and editors of mental health publications need to take special care to:

> make sure to think carefully and questioningly about the past and present claims made by those who "explain" human problems through mother-blame

> make sure to consider the entire range of potential causes of problems, both individual causes and social, political, and economic ones

> make sure to encourage examination of the damage done to mothers and their children through intensive and disproportionate mother-blame, as well as through making mothers disproportionately responsible for the care of their children

If the aim of science is to uncover the truth, then it is a modest proposal to suggest that all possible sources of trouble be considered and no single source be held disproportionately responsible.

It becomes especially clear how important this is when we consider the dramatic contrast between our culture's readiness to *blame* mothers for any problems in their children and its tendency to *excuse* men when they commit hurtful or violent acts.

# References

Caplan, P. J. (1989). *Don't blame mother: Mending the mother-daughter relationship.* New York: Harper & Row.

Caplan, P. J., & Hall-McCorquodale, I. (1985). Mother-blaming in major clinical journals. *American Journal of Orthopsychiatry, 55,* 345–353.

Nielsen, J., et al. (1970). Klinefelter's syndrome in children. *Journal of Child Psychology and Psychiatry, 11,* 109–119.

Sigal, J. (1976). Effects of paternal exposure to prolonged stress on the mental health of the spouse and children. *Canadian Psychiatric Association Journal, 21*(3), 169–172.

Smith, R., & Sharpe, T. (1970). Treatment of a school phobia with implosive therapy. *Journal of Consulting and Clinical Psychology, 35*(2), 239–242.

# DO HORMONES MAKE THE WOMAN?

It is widely believed that hormones, chemicals which are present in tiny amounts in our bodies, make women and men different not only in their genital and secondary-sex characteristics such as breasts, but also in their behavior and a wide range of their abilities. This belief has usually been to the detriment of women and girls; in regard to hormones, as in regard to so many sex differences, a *difference* has been misconstrued as a *female deficiency*.

We are told, on the one hand, that girls and women are *supposed* to be driven by hormones (to want to become pregnant, to take care of other people, to be emotionally expressive) and, on the other hand, that female hormones cause *overly* emotional, irrational, even crazy behavior. This is a perfect catch-22: The normal female is driven by her hormones, and female-hormone-impelled behavior is crazy; therefore the normal female is "naturally diseased" (Fausto-Sterling, 1985, p. 99), crazy—or at least irrational. Then, as biologist Anne Fausto-Sterling (1985) notes, it is concluded that "women, by nature emotionally erratic, cannot be trusted in positions of responsibility" (p. 91).

Even the passage of time does not help, for after they stop having periods, middle-aged postmenopausal women are still said to be abnormal (Fausto-Sterling, 1985). Their abnormality is alleged to be due to a *deficiency* in the very hormones that supposedly make *premenopausal* women irrational, but the consequences continue to be forms of emotional abnormality. As Fausto-Sterling puts it, "An unlikely specter haunts the world. It is the ghost of former womanhood" (p. 110). Fausto-Sterling quotes directly from descriptions of menopausal women offered by the so-called experts on menopause; allegedly characterized by their "vapid, cow-like negative state," the women are "unfortunate women abounding in the streets walking stiffly in twos and threes, seeing little and observing less. ... The world appears [to them] as through a grey veil, and they live as docile, harmless creatures missing most of life's values" (Wilson & Wilson, 1963, cited by Fausto-Sterling, 1985, p. 110).

Although these comments were made in 1963, similar attitudes pervade our culture even today. They are beginning to be recognized as both ageist and sexist, since they reflect the view that women who can no longer reproduce are less than womanly, less than human, in fact, pretty worthless and uninteresting.

Although there is ample documentation of the fact that people of *both* sexes experience hormonal variations and cycles, only those in women have been extensively used against them. This is partly because in a sexist society any evidence of difference is likely to be used to justify mistreatment of females. (There are important parallels, of course, in a racist society, an ageist society, and so on.) It is also partly because only females manifest a clear, known sign of a major hormonal change—monthly bleeding—and that makes females' hormonal cycles more salient.

In stark contrast to the way hormones are said to affect women negatively is the invocation of hormones to excuse males' negative behavior. As discussed in detail in Chapter 7 (Sex Differences in Aggression) males are widely regarded as unable to control their coercive sexual and aggressive, even violent behavior, because it is attributed to hormonal influences beyond their control.

Before looking in detail at issues related to the research on women's hormones, it is important to understand two basic, general principles about sex hormones. First, even the labeling of some hormones as "female" and others as "male" sets up a false dichotomy. Many people assume that only women have the "female" ones—estrogen and progesterone, and that only men have "male" hormones—androgens such as testosterone. This is a mistaken assumption which feeds the belief that males and females have totally different hormones and, therefore, totally different physical and behavioral characteristics. Both "male" and "female" hormones actually exist in both sexes. In fact, both sexes have testosterone in their bodies, but adult females have less of it in their blood than do adult males (Kutsky, 1981), and females and males have *receptors* that pick up the hormones from the bloodstream differentially. Thus, at puberty there are more observable effects of testosterone on males—development of their sex organs, increased body hair, deepened voice, and so on, but testosterone also stimulates early pubic hair growth and enlargement of the clitoris in females (Gadpaille, 1975; Villee, 1975).

A second basic principle relates to the question of cause and effect. Many laypeople and even some researchers assume that hormones lead to and affect behavior. This assumption feeds the belief that any sex differences we see in people's behavior are biologically based, and biologically based characteristics are usually assumed to be difficult, impossible, or even dangerous to modify. In fact, though, the process can go the opposite way: Behavior can change hormone levels. This subject was discussed in more detail in Chapter 7, but what is important here is to recognize that we should not readily attribute women's behavior to their hormones. Instead, for instance, such factors as women's learned attitudes about menstruation, their stress levels, and their athletic activity can change their hormonal levels.

Now we shall look at the most common phenomena attributed to women's hormones.

## ❖ WHAT COULD "PMS" BE?

It is said that, because of the hormonal variations occurring shortly before the menstrual period begins, women have major mood swings, become impossible to be around because they are so angry or depressed or both, and cannot think clearly or perform tasks as efficiently or competently as when they are not premenstrual. Various combinations of these "symptoms" have been called *premenstrual syndrome* or *PMS* by various authorities: "There is no one set of symptoms which is considered to be the hallmark of or standard criterion for defining the premenstrual syndrome" (Abplanalp, 1983, p. 110). We shall look first at what PMS is, then at some factors that make it hard to study relationships between hormones and emotions or behavior and, therefore, make it hard to find out whether something called PMS really exists as a discrete, identifiable entity.

Virtually every negative symptom—physical, emotional, and cognitive—has been called a premenstrual symptom by one or more clinicians or researchers at some time. Indeed, the range of physical and emotional changes associated with changes in women's biology has grown so wide it defies credibility. The symptoms of PMS have even been said to include alcoholism, suicide, perceptual problems, glaucoma, epilepsy, and allergies. Furthermore, so-called "PMS indicators" including "headaches, depression, dizziness, loss or gain of appetite show up in everyone from time to time. Their mere presence would not help one to diagnose the syndrome" (Fausto-Sterling, 1985, p. 97; see her chapter, Hormonal Hurricanes, for a brilliant review). Although hormones are known to have some physical and emotional effects, it is hard to imagine that everything negative that women do or that happens to women is due to hormonal changes—and that the same is *not* true for men.

These problems of definition and classification make it impossible to answer the question, "Is there such a thing as PMS, and if so, what is it?" because nearly every researcher or research team has had its own, idiosyncratic definition of PMS. In other words, as with research on "spatial abilities" (see Chapter 4), although researchers often give the impression that there *is* such a thing as PMS, and that their work is an attempt to discover its exact nature, that is not the case. Like spatial abilities, "PMS" is a construct, a label that was created and used as though it applies to a known entity, even though the scientists who study "it" cannot even agree on what its definition should be. Thus, to try to inspect the PMS literature and draw conclusions about what PMS might be is a fruitless task, because it is somewhat like trying to add together research on horses, nuts and bolts, and caffeine.

Before even looking at the research on PMS, it is important to remember that negative behavior that is thought to be physically caused is usually considered hard to change or even unchangeable. Some people go so far as to claim that physically caused behavior—especially when it involves a sex differ-ence—*should not* be changed, that that would be "tampering with nature." So unless there is compelling, reliable evidence from scrupulously conducted research to support the claim that females' hormones make them irrational and undependable, it is very dangerous to perpetuate the myth of PMS and thus the myth that women are inevitably irrational and disturbed.

It is crucial to keep in mind that menstrual periods in North America and many other countries are embedded in a host of fearful and shameful feelings (Golub, 1985). As a result, it is difficult for young girls to grow up having sim-ply positive feelings about menstruation, and thus they might indeed become upset each month just before their periods begin. Some researchers have found that women's negative feelings were "more responsive to the presence of stressful external events than to the specific timing of the menstrual cycle phase" (Friedman et al., 1980, p. 722), and social taboos about menstruation are one source of stress. Indeed, a great many social factors may lead to pre-menstrual symptoms. For instance, it has been found that "premenstrual increases in anxiety were characteristic of women with normal to heavy men-strual flow" (Friedman et al., 1980, p. 723). It may be that women find heavy bleeding to be inconvenient, potentially embarrassing, or physically uncom-fortable or painful, and this makes them feel irritable when their periods are due. Similarly, Brooks, Ruble, and Clark (1977) found that "reports of increased negative affect during the menstrual phase were associated with the view of menstruation as a debilitating and predictable event" (Friedman et al., 1980, p. 723). Furthermore, Carol Tavris (1992) has observed that the eras in which PMS has been regarded as a problem or an illness have tended to be those in which there have been the strongest efforts to keep women down and keep them out of the workplace.

This is not to say that hormonal changes at some points—or perhaps at several points—in the menstrual cycle cannot ever have negative consequences *apart from* social factors. Indeed, there is increasing evidence that women who have had tubal ligations (have had "their tubes tied"), and who had nothing they considered PMS before the surgery, have begun to have upsetting symp-toms premenstrually after the ligation has been done (Cattanach, 1985; *PMS Information and Referral Newsletter,* 1987). And in some other cases women may report suffering anywhere from moderately to a great deal because of hor-monal changes, which *can* affect both moods and bodies. However, to say that hormones themselves may be troublesome for a small proportion of women is very different from the claim that nearly all women (physicians in a typical study said from 25 to 100 percent!: O'Connor, Edward, & Stern, 1974) have major emotional problems because of the hormones that "make them female."

Whatever the cause of distressing premenstrual changes, it is striking that the American Psychiatric Association, in its official handbook of disorders, has chosen to call women's (allegedly) hormonally based mood changes a psy-chiatric disorder but has no category at all for *men's* hormonally based mood changes (American Psychiatric Association, 1987). This is a particularly seri-ous omission in view of the fact that only a tiny proportion of women (whether premenstrual or not) *ever* display the level of violence that is displayed by large proportions of men (Russell, 1982, 1984). That *is* a striking sex difference, and if it turned out to be due to hormonal factors, then it would seem even more important to label men's dangerous, hormonally based behavior than women's irritability or depression as a serious problem.

Koeske (1987; see also Koeske & Koeske, 1975; Koeske, 1975) found that observers of other people's behavior attributed only negative behavior to women's biology. If people were told someone who behaved positively was premenstrual, they interpreted this as a result of personality or situational influences. They also found that when negative behavior was attributed to a woman's being premenstrual, the same behavior was rated as more extreme and unreasonable than when a man or nonpremenstrual woman did the same thing (Koeske, 1987). This illustrates the mechanism that keeps a stereotype in place. For example, if it is considered "unnatural" for a woman to be angry, then there must be a biological explanation for her angry behavior: She must be "sick."

## ❖ WHY IT'S HARD TO INVESTIGATE HORMONALLY CAUSED PROBLEMS

The definitional problems discussed above constitute a major obstacle to studying "PMS." Many other problems plague that area of research, and some of those are characteristic of *any* attempt to link hormones with behavior (including emotions and abilities or performance). There is no room here to cover all of these problems, but we shall give a sampling of them, followed by an example of how some of the problems appear in one study.

In regard to PMS in particular, Fausto-Sterling provides an excellent summary of the research roadblocks related to the time period studied:

> PMS research usually bases itself on an ideal, regular, twenty-eight-day menstrual cycle. Researchers eliminate as subjects for study women with infrequent, shorter, or longer cycles. As a result, published investigations look at a skewed segment of the overall population. Even for those women with a regular cycle, however, a methodological problem remains because few researchers define the premenstrual period in the same way. Some studies look only at the day or two preceding the menstrual flow, others look at the week preceding, [and some] cite cases that begin two weeks before menstruation and continue for one week after. (1985, p. 98)

The issue of timing also affects the study of menopausal changes. For instance, should researchers define menopause as beginning with the first missed menstrual period? The first late one? The first one in which the flow is somewhat reduced (which may occur years before the first missed period)? And, of course, all of these timing issues become even thornier in women whose periods have always been irregular.

The reason that timing is so important in studying hormonal effects is that many researchers assume that increases or decreases in one or more hormones lead to behavioral or emotional changes. If all women had regular cycles, this kind of research would be easier to do, but that is not the case. Cycles vary from one woman to another. Some women are very regular, and others are not. The truth is that without doing blood tests or some other careful measurements, it is not possible to know for sure just how much of a particular hormone is present in a person's body at any time. One way to try to get around this problem, rather than unjustifiably assuming that all the participants in a study follow identical hormonal patterns over each month, would be to take daily blood samples from all women in a research study, measure the levels of all hormones in those samples, and see whether they correlate with behavioral or emotional changes. However, there are practical problems finding the time and money to hire staff to draw daily blood samples and finding enough participants who have the time, energy, and willingness to show up every day. Furthermore, it can be stressful to be stuck frequently with a needle, and changes in stress levels are known to affect hormone production. Finally, daily blood sampling would make it difficult to conceal from the women the fact that something about their physiology is the subject of study, and there is no way to know how that might skew the results.

Other problems in research on women's hormones include "inadequate sample sizes and measures, inappropriate choice of subjects, tests designed to obtain a desired outcome, and poor or nonexistent use of statistical analysis" (Fausto-Sterling, 1985, p. 101), as well as the unreliability of retrospective reports (Parlee, 1973). Caplan, McCurdy-Myers, and Gans (1992) have noted still more methodological shortcomings, including the fact that the PMS label itself is scientifically unsound; the difficulty of gathering relevant data without the participants being aware of the purpose of the study and thus perhaps skewing the results; the difficulty of finding out to what extent a person's *report* of changes in their moods or behavior actually correspond to those changes; small numbers of participants in many studies; researchers' sloppiness in checking on the exact timing and course of the women's menstrual cycles; and unreliable or inadequate measures of mood, behavior, or other "symptoms."

Even Katharina Dalton, a firm believer in the existence and pervasiveness of PMS, has identified many problems in studying it: variations in menstrual cycle length for the same and different women (which makes it difficult to tell which stage of the cycle women are at when studied, and calls into question the concept of a "typical" cycle); the difficulty of telling what effect hormones have, since women vary in their response to stress, age, parenthood, medical history, use of birth control, attitudes toward pregnancy, and so on; and the difficulty of deciding how to select the women who are to be compared to women with PMS (what is a "normal" woman if most women are alleged to have PMS?) (Dalton, 1987).

Many similar problems plague the research on menopause. One particularly problematic research error has been investigators' mistaken assumption that menopause involves the *absence* of estrogen. However, it does not; it involves only a "gradual lowering in the availability of *ovarian* estrogen," and not necessarily a change in estrogen elsewhere (Fausto-Sterling, 1985, pp. 114–115). Indeed, there are several forms of estrogen, most of which after menopause continue to be produced at a level "comparable to that observed during the early phases of the menstrual cycle" (Fausto-Sterling, 1985, p. 115). In spite of this, researchers continue to search energetically for a single and simple cause-effect relationship between a change in the level of one hormone (or perhaps two) and such symptoms as hot flashes or a decrease in vaginal lubrication. And most of the research on treatments for allegedly menopause-related problems involves the use of estrogen only or only estrogen and progesterone. The fact that the nature and pattern of hormonal changes at menopause vary enormously from woman to woman is rarely considered.

To illustrate how some of the methodological problems come into play, we shall look in some detail at the work of Rudolph Moos, who developed the Menstrual Distress Questionnaire (MDQ) (1968) as a method of evaluating the effects of hormones on women. To develop the questionnaire, he asked 839 wives of male graduate students to describe the menstrual, premenstrual, and intermenstrual phases of their worst menstrual cycle and of their most recent menstrual cycle. The women were then asked to rate 47 symptoms on a 6-point scale, ranging from "no experience of the symptom" to "acute or partially disabling experience of the symptoms." Of the 47 symptoms, 3 were fairly neutral ("change in eating habits," "stay at home," and "orderliness"), and 4 were positive (e.g., "affectionate"). The other 40 items were negative, covering a range of physical and mental problems (e.g., "chest pains," "headache," "decreased efficiency," "crying"). Moos reported that he found "approximately 30–50% of normal young married women are bothered to some extent by cyclical symptoms of cramps, backache, headache, irritability, mood swings, tension and/or depression" (Moos, 1968, p. 863).

Let us now consider what this information tells us about the validity of Moos's work. First, the young wives of male graduate students cannot be said to represent the population of women as a whole, for the former are probably younger and better-educated than the average woman. (He doesn't tell us whether the young women are graduate students themselves.) We won't know how that could affect the women's reporting of symptoms until a great deal more research is done; however, as one example, younger women might report fewer symptoms because menstruation is a less taboo subject for them than for women of earlier generations. So Moos's results really might apply only to young women who are married to graduate students. In fact, the sample is further limited because all of these women were living in university housing at a large western university in the United States. So the results cannot even be assumed to apply to all young women who are married to graduate students.

Next, rather than requesting that the women keep a record of their feelings, Moos asked them to remember how they experienced 47 feelings at three different points during each of two months. This is an enormous demand on memory, and there is no way in his study to determine whether or not their recollections were accurate. This is all the more problematic because their "worst" cycle might have been years before. Moos assumed also that all 839 women *knew* when they were premenstrual and intermenstrual, and how their feelings corresponded to their hormones, but he did not attempt to check out his assumptions. This is particularly crucial for women with irregular cycles.

Rating moods can, of course, only be done from the point of view of the person having them, which makes it difficult to tell what these ratings mean. Does each woman who rates her depression at "three" mean or experience the same thing as every other woman who chooses the same rating?

By asking women to report on their feelings during their menstrual cycle as if these reports proved that hormonal changes affected their feelings, Moos assumed that women were not influenced by widespread stereotypes about how women's hormones affect them or by other factors. Can a woman be sure that her feelings are a result of hormonal changes? A woman could arrive at a definition of her "worst" menstrual cycle by reasoning: "I felt very angry, so I must have been having a bad case of premenstrual tension." Because Moos is questioning her about the effect of her hormones on her feelings, she may not recall that this was the week when the sink backed up, it was 95 degrees outside, and the neighbor played loud music all night long; or, if she could recall those factors, the task Moos gave her may make it less likely that she will attribute her anger to anything other than PMS. Also, a woman might feel depressed and so on, because she is premenstrual and knows the stereotype.

Mary Brown Parlee (1974) has pointed out that Moos's questionnaire items are heavily biased toward negative experiences, although some women experience no changes or even increased energy and zest premenstrually. Parlee also reports that responses to the MDQ have not been shown to be reliable for the same woman two cycles in a row (1974). This makes it difficult to judge whether a woman's responses have any consistent relationship to her hormonal changes. Furthermore, Parlee points out that some items on the questionnaire, such as "distractible," are not very clearly defined, and different women could interpret them in very different ways.

Parlee (1974) wondered whether changes in feelings during the course of a month are necessarily due to women's hormonal changes or whether women have simply learned to attribute the changes to their hormones. So, she asked both women and men to use the MDQ to describe what women experience during the menstrual cycle. She found that "men and women report virtually identical patterns of symptoms and symptom changes" (p. 239). Males agreed with females about which symptoms changed the most in women during the menstrual cycle, which changed second most, and so on. When the males' answers were significantly different from those of the females, that was because males rated the symptoms as more severe than did the females (p. 235). This strongly suggests that the questionnaire measures stereotypic beliefs about menstruation rather than actual changes due to hormonal fluctuations (Parlee, 1974, p. 239).

### ❖ THE CHOICE OF RESEARCH QUESTION

Throughout most of this chapter, the focus has been on specific dilemmas, errors, and confusion in investigating what are assumed to be women's hormonally caused problems. But with this topic, as with many others, it is very revealing to step way back and ask, "Why is this such a popular research topic? Why is so much energy invested in allegedly exploring what's wrong with *women?*"

The vast power of the connection in many people's minds between female hormones and the inability to think clearly or perform important tasks is reflected in the words of the physician to former Vice President Hubert Humphrey in 1970; referring to these hormonal differences, that doctor, Edgar Berman, wrote to a woman member of the United States Congress:

> Even a Congresswoman must defer to scientific truths . . . there just are physical and psychological inhibitants that limit a female's potential. . . . I would still rather have a male John F. Kennedy make the Cuban missile crisis decisions than a female of the same age who could possibly be subject to the curious mental aberrations of that age group. (Berman, 1970)

Since Berman wrote those words, it has become less socially acceptable to make such claims explicitly and publicly, but informally and behind closed doors where important decisions about politics and careers are made, such ideas are still frequently expressed. And such concerns give rise to research.

Since not only women's but also men's hormones have been shown to follow cyclical patterns, why should nearly all of the research on the possible relationships between hormones and behavior be focused on women? For instance, it has been suggested that women shouldn't be allowed to pilot airplanes, since they could be poor pilots during their premenstrual times. However, *even if* it were true that some women have something like PMS that does hamper their performance of piloting tasks, at least—even for those women—we could predict on which days they shouldn't fly planes. But for men, unless we check their hormone levels by doing daily blood tests, we don't know when *their* piloting ability might be hampered by hormonal factors. Therefore, it would seem logical that if there were to be a major research effort in this area, it ought to be aimed at learning more about men! It is fascinating that cycles in men's hormones have been documented, as have cycles in men's behaviour (Steinem 1992). In fact, when male railway train engineers' workdays were determined according to 28-day cycles, the number of accidents "was cut more drastically than it had been by any other measure" (Steinem, 1992, p. 291).

What this example illustrates is the highly political nature of sex-difference research. The focus has been on women's hormones rather than men's because women are regarded as "at the mercy of their hormones," as emotionally uncontrolled, whereas men are not. This seems particularly strange in view of the theory that *men's* testosterone makes *them* incapable of controlling their sexual and aggressive feelings. In other words, research on "how women are controlled by their hormones" fits with the prevailing social belief that women have less self-control than men. Therefore, women have been *kept out of* powerful positions *on account of* their alleged hormonally based undependability, but men are *allowed to* run countries and fly airplanes, *in spite of* their allegedly hormonally based, uncontrollable aggression. Research that fits with widely accepted beliefs has historically been more likely to receive financial support, to receive moral support from the researcher's peers, and to be accepted for publication in scholarly journals than research that goes against prevailing beliefs.

Therefore, when looking at any piece of sex-difference research, it is important to ask whether that particular research question is being asked because it helps confirm common beliefs and whether quite different questions might give us more important information.

# References

Abplanalp, J. (1983). Premenstrual syndrome: A selective review. *Women and Health, 8*, 107–123.

Berman, E. (1970, July 26). Letter to the editor. *New York Times.*

Brooks, J.; Ruble, D. N.; & Clark, A.E. (1977). College women's attitudes and expectations concerning menstrual-related changes. *Psychosomatic Medicine, 39,* 288–298.

Caplan, P. J.; McCurdy-Myers, J.; & Gans, M. (1992). Should PMS be called a psychiatric abnormality? *Feminism and Psychology, 2,* 27–44.

Cattanach, J. (1985, April 13). Estrogen deficiency after tubal ligation. *Lancet,* 847–849.

Dalton, K. (1987). What is this PMS? In M. R. Walsh (Ed.), *The psychology of women: Ongoing debates* (pp. 131–136). New Haven: Yale University Press.

Fausto-Sterling, A. (1985). *Myths of gender: Biological theories about women and men.* New York: Basic Books.

Friedman, R. C., et al. (1980). Behavior and the menstrual cycle. *Signs, 5,* 719–738.

Gadpaille, W. (1975). *The cycles of sex.* New York: Charles Scribner's Sons.

Golub, S. (1985). *Lifting the curse of menstruation: A feminist appraisal of the influence of menstruation in women's lives.* New York: Harrington Park Press.

Koeske, R. (1987). Premenstrual emotionality: Is biology destiny? In M. R. Walsh (Ed.), *The psychology of women: Ongoing debates* (pp. 137–146). New Haven: Yale University Press.

Koeske, R. (1975). *"Premenstrual tension" as an explanation of female hostility.* Paper presented at American Psychological Association convention.

Koeske, R., & Koeske, G.F. (1975). An attributional approach to moods and the menstrual cycle. *Journal of Personality and Social Psychology, 3,* 473–478.

Kutsky, R. J. (1981). *Handbook of vitamins, minerals, and hormones.* New York: Van Nostrand Reinhold.

Moos, R. (1968). The development of a Menstrual Distress Questionnaire. *Psychosomatic Medicine, 30,* 853–867.

O'Connor, J.; Edward, M. S.; & Stern, L. O. (1974). Behavioral rhythms related to the menstrual cycle. In M. Ferin (Ed.), *Biorhythms and human reproduction.* New York: Wiley.

Parlee, M. B . (1973). The premenstrual syndrome. *Psychological Bulletin, 80,* 454–465.

Parlee, M. B. (1974). Stereotypic beliefs about menstruation: A methodological note on the Moos Menstrual Distress Questionnaire and some new data. *Psychosomatic Medicine, 36,* 229–240.

*PMS information and referral newsletter.* Report of June 25, 1987, meeting (Box 363, Station L; Toronto, Ontario M6E 4Z3 Canada).

Russell, D. E. H. (1982). *Rape in marriage.* New York: Macmillan.

Russell, D. E. H. (1984). *Sexual exploitation: Rape, child sexual abuse, and workplace harassment.* Beverly Hills: Sage.

Steinem, G. (1992). *Revolution from within: A book of self-esteem.* Boston: Little, Brown.

Tavris, C. (1992). *The mismeasure of woman.* New York: Simon & Schuster.

Villee, D. (1975). *Human endocrinology: A developmental approach.* Philadelphia: Saunders.

Wilson, R. A., & Wilson, T. (1963). The fate of the nontreated postmenopausal woman: A plea for the maintenance of adequate estrogen from puberty to the grave. *Journal of the American Geriatric Society, 11,* 352–356.

## CHAPTER
## TEN

# DO FEMALES HAVE BETTER VERBAL ABILITIES THAN MALES?

I t is widely believed that females' verbal abilities are superior to those of males. Both laypeople and researchers often act as though this is true. For instance, many parents expect their daughters to begin to speak or read earlier or perform better on spelling tests than their sons. And in the realm of research, in a classic book, *The Psychology of Sex Differences*, authors Maccoby and Jacklin (1974) state: "Female superiority on verbal tasks has been one of the more solidly established generalizations in the field of sex differences" (p. 75). They report a similar conclusion in their book under the heading of "Sex Differences That Are Fairly Well Established" (p. 351).

In view of the many arenas in which males are said to be superior, it might seem surprising to discover one in which a superiority is reported for females. However, this arena is often interpreted as an undesirable one, even one deserving of mockery. For instance, instead of talking about "females' superior verbal abilities," one often hears people deride girls and women for talking too much or about trivial matters, never knowing when to keep quiet, or being unable to keep a secret. In the nineteenth century, too, as psychologist Catherine Gildiner explains in her paper, "Science as a political weapon: A study of the nineteenth-century sex difference literature" (1977), when the data themselves were not challenged, they were transformed into ways to discredit or demean women. As noted in Chapter 2:

> In relation to the . . . finding of women's ability to read faster, Lombroso and Ferrero . . . pointed out that [t]his finding should not come as the shock to the scientific community that it apparently did. They pointed out that women

had a greater rapidity of perception but what accompanies such a trait is also a trait for "lying" that is "almost pathological." (Gildiner, 1977, p. 82)

The linking of women's greater verbal abilities to lying, as was done in the previous century, may seem quaint, naive, and unjustifiably damaging to women; however, it is not really so different when people today associate women's supposed verbal superiority with such other demeaned forms of behavior as talking too much or indiscreetly. Wine, Moses, and Smye (1980) describe how a reviewer of the research on verbal abilities found another way to demean females' alleged verbal superiority: He carefully selected which studies he would cite and then labeled the verbal skills on which girls were said to excel as "lower level" ones while calling those verbal skills on which boys were said to excel "higher level" ones (Lynn, 1972).

These examples illustrate the way an alleged female superiority becomes transformed into still another apparent female inferiority through treatment of the relevant abilities as undesirable. But even when the abilities are regarded as desirable—as with reading and spelling—the practical consequences are often hurtful to females. Reading and spelling disabilities have long been reported as far more common in male children (Kinsbourne & Caplan, 1979, summarize these reports), and as psychologist Meredith Kimball has pointed out, far more tax money has gone into providing special classes and learning materials for children with reading and spelling disabilities than for those with spatial or mathematical disabilities, which are said to be more common among females (see Chapter 4 and Chapter 10 for further discussion of these topics).

In one study in which adults were asked to decide which children on a list of students needing tutoring help should get top priority, adults of both sexes regarded boys, especially those with reading problems, as needing help more urgently than girls or than children with problems in doing arithmetic (Caplan, 1977). This might mean that boys' reading problems are more likely than girls' to be noticed. In a similar vein, Caplan and Kinsbourne (1974) speculated that girls with reading problems might be overlooked because girls are taught to deal quietly with failure, whereas boys are allowed to cope with failure in more aggressive, disruptive ways that would draw teachers' attention to them. Indeed, Shaywitz, Shaywitz, Fletcher, and Escobar (1990) have now discovered that learning disabilities are *not* more common among boys than among girls but *are* more commonly *noticed and diagnosed* in boys.

The fact that verbal abilities, however they are valued or devalued, are said to be an area of *female* superiority should not prevent us from asking exactly the same kinds of critical questions that we ask about male-superiority areas. So, we shall ask, as we did about spatial abilities:

1. What are *verbal abilities*? or How has the term been defined, used, and tested?

2. *Are* there sex differences in verbal abilities? If so, how big are they?

3. Why have people believed there are such big sex differences in these abilities?

## ❖ WHAT ARE VERBAL ABILITIES?

As we noted in Chapter 4 with regard to "spatial abilities," in an important sense there are no such things as verbal abilities: People invented the term *verbal abilities*, and many different people use it in many different ways. When we hear someone say, "That student is verbally skilled," we tend to believe we know what that means. But unless everyone has in mind the same, precise definition or the same list of tests that measure "verbal abilities," then in fact we do *not* all agree about its meaning.

As with "spatial abilities," researchers who report that they have studied sex differences in "verbal abilities" rarely define the term. Most often, they simply tell what test or tests they used to measure "verbal abilities." Virtually never do they even address the question: "Are there several or multiple components of verbal abilities, or do all 'verbal' tests tap a single, general ability?" A list of the "verbal" abilities measured on such tests in recent decades includes, but is not limited to, the following: vocabulary size; speed of reading; reading comprehension; ability to express an idea in the fewest possible words; ability to make a number of different words from a group of letters; frequency of initiating conversations; ability to memorize lists of unrelated words quickly; ability to read, write, understand, and/or speak a foreign language; understanding of analogies; creative writing; fluency; age when speaking first word or first sentence; age when making first sound with the throat, tongue, or lips; skill at playing such word games as Hangman; amount of spontaneous production of sounds by infants, while awake or asleep; toddlers' talk to other children; toddlers' making of play noises; children's talking to themselves while performing tasks; children's requests for information from their mothers; children's following of instructions; children's mimicry of nonsense or meaningful words; use of incomplete sentences; adults' use of "ah"s; ability to learn a code; color-naming skill; choice of pictures after hearing descriptive sentences; skill at doing anagrams; use of plural noun formations; length of sentences; errors in similes; free associations; and descriptions of abstract pictures and pictures of faces (many of these come from reviews and tables by Maccoby & Jacklin, 1974, and the others come from Ho, 1987; Pepin, Beaulieu, Matte, & Leroux, 1985; Waber, 1977; Wilkie & Eisdorfer, 1977).

As with the research on spatial abilities, in individual studies of verbal abilities, any given researcher has tested one or more of those listed, but no one has tested them all. And in another parallel with spatial abilities research, it is clear that many of these skills involve more than verbal abilities (whatever they are). For example, children's following of instructions could tap not only their ability to understand spoken words but also their inclination to be compliant. Similarly, the length of people's sentences could depend not only on their verbal fluency but also on their shyness, familiarity with the experimenter or teacher, and a host of other factors. In other words, it is hard to find a "pure" test, one that measures *only* verbal abilities. It is also an overwhelming task to give a single group of people all possible tests that might reveal the true picture of whatever "verbal abilities" are.

No single authority has concluded "Verbal abilities consist solely and completely of X and Y, and here are the tests that measure them" and then found that other researchers all agreed. Therefore, the term "verbal abilities" continues to be used in many ways. If a scientist reports a finding about "verbal abilities," we need to know whether that scientist based the finding on a test of only one specific type of verbal ability and is claiming to have found a sex difference in "verbal abilities" or has tested a variety of abilities. When we read that a difference has been found in "verbal abilities," it is essential that we *not* assume that the difference has been found in *all* of what might be considered to be verbal abilities.

Now, if all of these tests yielded the same conclusion (for instance, that females are more skilled than males), the number and variety of tests might not be so problematic. We might feel that we need not worry too much about defining the term precisely, if all of the tests that people call "verbal" showed a female superiority. But, as we shall see in the next section, that is not the case.

In trying to test for verbal abilities, we encounter another problem if we want to find out whether there might be an *innate* sex difference: We don't want to test children when they are very old, since by then boys and girls have been treated differently for so long and in so many ways. Thus, if we found sex differences even in 6-year-olds, it would be hard to conclude that they were innate.

It would appear, then, that we need to test people as young as possible. But how does one test "verbal abilities" in newborns, since they do not speak? How does one measure verbal abilities at the beginning of life? Some researchers have measured what they believe to be the "precursors" of verbal abilities, the behavior that leads to or gives rise to actual speech; for instance, they might measure how many nonword sounds infants make in their throats. But infants who make many nonword sounds do not necessarily become children who speak early or adults who know a lot of word definitions.

In conclusion, it appears that there is no agreement about what is meant by the term *verbal abilities*, even though many people believe that females are better at those abilities than are males.

## ✦ ARE THERE SEX DIFFERENCES IN VERBAL ABILITIES?

One of the most important points about the research on sex differences in verbal abilities is that *most published studies show NO sex difference.* In Maccoby and Jacklin's (1974) review of a massive number of studies, they reached the conclusion that there was a female superiority in verbal abilities *even though* their own description of the studies reveals the following:

Of experiments about "spontaneous vocal and verbal behavior," in 19 studies there was no sex difference, in 8 there was a female superiority, and in 2 there was a male superiority.

Of experiments about verbal abilities on actual tests, in 81 studies there was no sex difference, in 37 there was a female superiority, and in 13 there was a male superiority.

In our own review of studies published since the Maccoby and Jacklin book appeared, we found no substantial difference in that pattern. Furthermore, it is well known that studies in which no sex difference appears are far less likely to be accepted and published by journal editors than are studies that yield a difference (Caplan, 1979). Therefore, if all of the unpublished, no-difference studies of verbal abilities could be located and added to the statistics, the proportion showing a sex difference of any kind would probably be even smaller. But even if we decided (unreasonably) to ignore the no-difference studies, do we feel comfortable concluding on the basis of, say, 45 studies that females have a verbal superiority? What do we make of the, say, 15 studies that reveal a male superiority? Do we act as though they tell us nothing at all, just because there are more of the former?

Another important point is that it is hard to know how to interpret all of the available data combined. Some researchers have made attempts, through fairly sophisticated statistical techniques, to see how all the data look when they are put together (meta-analysis discussed in Chapter 3). However, the studies vary enormously in the numbers of people tested (in Maccoby and Jacklin's review, for instance, the numbers ranged from a low of 4 people to a high of 238,145!) and in their ages (in Maccoby and Jacklin's review, the range was from 2 weeks to 84 years of age), their geographical place of origin and their urban or rural location, their levels of education, and their races and social classes. In fact, in regard to race, social class, and education, researchers often fail to report this information in their articles.

Studies also differ greatly in the ways they measure verbal abilities, as noted earlier. How, then, can we compare a study, for instance, of the foreign language skills of 230 undergraduates from Hong Kong (Ho, 1987) to one of the ability of 56 preteen and teenage children to play the spelling game of Hangman (Pepin et al., 1985) to one of the ability of 64 people between the ages of 60 and 79 years to memorize lists of unrelated words? Since we simply do not know whether the Hong Kong undergraduates' foreign language abilities are good predictors of how well they will memorize unrelated words when they are between 60 and 79 years of age, would we really want to combine the results of these two studies in drawing a conclusion about sex differences in something called "verbal abilities"? And the dilemma becomes even more complicated when we realize (Maccoby & Jacklin, 1974) that within some studies, males do better at some tasks called "verbal," and females do better on other tasks which are also called "verbal"; indeed, sometimes a sex difference is reversed or disappears depending on which *subtest* of a particular test is given (Maccoby & Jacklin, 1974). How, then, should we interpret those?

A third important issue related to the question of sex differences in verbal abilities is that when differences have appeared, they have tended to be extremely small. In fact, they are strikingly similar to those reported for spatial abilities (see Chapter 4). In Chapter 4, we pointed out that when only 1–5 percent of the *variance* is accounted for by sex, that means that "if you wanted to predict whether someone would score high or low on a . . . test, knowing their sex would give you only between 1 and 5 percent . . . of the information you would need in order to make a correct prediction. In other words, sex may sometimes play a role in one's score, but that role is tiny" (p. 32, in this book). The same is true for verbal abilities. Psychologist Hilary Lips, in her book *Sex and Gender: An Introduction* (1988), explains that research done by Janet Shibley Hyde (1981) "showed that gender accounted for an average of only 1% on the variance in verbal performance scores. Other reviewers have come to the same conclusion: Knowing a person's gender allows us to predict very little about that person's verbal ability (Plomin & Foch, 1981)" (p. 124).

When the differences are that small, it also means that there is an enormous amount of overlap between the scores of females and those of males. This is crucial to remember because, as discussed in Chapter 1, when people talk about sex differences, for most of us this calls up an image of the sexes being very different from each other, with little or no overlap.

A final point about the small size of those rarely found differences is that, as with spatial abilities, the difference could amply be accounted for by the enormous sex differences in social influences on and expectations of females in contrast to males. In other words, it is hard to use those data to justify the claim that there is an *innate* sex difference in verbal abilities.

## ❖ PROBLEMS WITH TEST CONSTRUCTION

Even when a sex difference in verbal abilities is found, it is hard to know what to make of it because of the way tests are constructed. Research is regarded with such awe that we often forget that tests are not objective instruments designed by machines to tell the Truth! Instead, people have to choose what kinds of questions go into any given test. Although some test designers use sophisticated statistical procedures to help decide which items to keep and which to throw out as they develop and refine their tests, it is impossible to get rid of the human element, and therefore it is impossible to get rid of bias and error. Let us look at an example which has profoundly important effects on the lives of millions of people: the SAT, which is used in North America and elsewhere to evaluate applicants to colleges and universities.

In order to understand a major problem with the SAT's Verbal Test (SAT-V), consider this question: If you are designing a test, and you discover that on some questions, people of one sex usually score higher than people of the other sex, what should you do? Should you eliminate all such items, or should you leave them in? If you eliminate them so that the test won't appear sex-biased due to repeatedly yielding higher scores for students of one sex than for students of the other, then you might be covering up a *real* sex difference in performance. What if there is an innate difference in that ability? Or, what if there is a sex difference in performance on those questions because one sex is discouraged from developing the relevant ability (e.g., boys are often discouraged from reading and learning about poetry)? Then, if your test covers up that difference, the sex that needs extra help or encouragement will be less likely to receive it.

On the other hand, if you leave such items in the test, the sex difference in performance may result *not* from a real sex difference in "verbal abilities" (whatever they are) but from the *way* those abilities are connected to other material on your test. For instance, in the SAT-V test, it has been shown that females score higher on reading comprehension and interpretation items when the paragraphs are about human relations, arts, and humanities, but boys score higher when the paragraphs are about science and business (Alington & Leaf, 1991). Does that show that one sex is better verbally than the other or that *everyone's* verbal abilities are revealed at their best when they work on topics with which they feel comfortable?

Alington and Leaf (1991) reported not only that females and males performed differently depending on the content of the SAT-V questions but also that in the 1960s females did better than males, but by the 1980s males were doing better than females (Dwyer, 1976). They found that fewer human relations, arts, and humanities items were used in the 1960s and more science and business ones in the 1980s. Clearly, the SAT-V is not a *pure* test of verbal abilities and verbal abilities alone. Thus, what would happen if, as with most sex-difference research, we decided to examine sex differences in verbal abilities by testing all 17-year-olds in a single year? If we had done that in the 1960s, we would probably have thought we had discovered a female superiority, but if we had done that in the 1980s, we would have thought we had discovered the reverse.

## ❖ WHY HAVE SOME PEOPLE BELIEVED IN FEMALES' VERBAL SUPERIORITY?

We can only speculate about why so many people believe in females' verbal superiority when the data do not justify it. Two possibilities come to mind, however. One is that women have often been criticized and mocked for "talking too much," and that has made it fairly easy to misconstrue data about superiority in important verbal abilities as proof that women never stop talking or that they nag or use words to control and manipulate men and children. In fact, however, as Dale Spender (1980) and Gloria Steinem (1983) point out, one reason it seems that women talk a lot is that they have traditionally been expected to keep silent. A woman who speaks up, and speaks her mind, is still in greater danger than a man of being regarded as overly aggressive and acting inappropriately.

A second possibility is that the (unjustified) belief that males have more learning disabilities has fed the belief in females' verbal superiority.

We have seen that vast improvements must be made in clarifying the meaning of "verbal abilities," in designing tests, and in carrying out and interpreting studies before we can draw any definite conclusions about sex differences in verbal abilties. To the media and the public, however, the indeterminacy of the research is not so apparent. The fact is that in the past (and even now), people have wrongly assumed that the minimal differences sometimes obtained on some of the tests are significant and dependable, as with spatial and math abilities.

# References

Alington, D. E., & Leaf, R. C. (1991). Elimination of SAT-Verbal sex differences was due to policy-guided changes in item content. *Psychological Reports, 68,* 541–542.

Caplan, P. J. (1979). Beyond the box score: A boundary condition for sex differences in aggression and achievement striving. In B. Maher (Ed). *Progress in Experimental Personality Research 9* (pp. 41–87).

Caplan, P. J. (1977). Sex, age, behavior, and school subject as determinants of report of learning problems. *Journal of Learning Disabilities, 10,* 314–316.

Caplan, P. J., & Kinsbourne, M. (1974). Sex differences in response to school failure. *Journal of Learning Disabilities, 4,* 232–235.

Dwyer, C. A. (1976). *Test content in mathematics and science: The consideration of sex.* Paper presented at American Educational Research Association, San Francisco.

Gildiner, C. (1977). *Science as a political weapon: A study of the nineteenth century sex differences literature.* York University. Downsview, Ontario.

Ho, D. Y. F. (1987). Prediction of foreign language skills: A canonical and part canonical correlation study. *Contemporary Educational Psychology, 12,* 119–130.

Hyde, J. S. (1981). How large are cognitive gender differences? A meta-analysis using $\Omega^2$ and d. *American Psychologist, 36,* 892–901.

Kinsbourne, M., & Caplan, P. J. (1979). *Children's learning and attention problems.* Boston: Little, Brown.

Lips, H. (1988). *Sex and gender: An introduction.* Mountain View, CA: Mayfield.

Lynn, D. B. (1972). Determinants of intellectual growth in women. *School Review, 80,* 241–260.

Maccoby, E. E., & Jacklin, C. N. (1974). *The psychology of sex differences.* Stanford, CA: Stanford University Press.

Pepin, M.; Beaulieu, R.; Matte, R.; & Leroux, Y. (1985). Microcomputer games and sex-related differences: Spatial, verbal, and mathematical abilities. *Psychological Reports, 56,* 783–786.

Plomin, R., & Foch, T. (1981). Sex differences and individual differences. *Child Development, 52,* 383–385.

Shaywitz, S. E.; Shaywitz, B. A.; Fletcher, J. M.; & Escobar, M. (1990) Prevalence of reading disability in boys and girls: Results of the Connecticut longitudinal study. *Journal of American Medical Association, 264*(8), 998–1002.

Spender, D. (1980). *Man made language.* London: Routledge & Kegan Paul.

Steinem, G. (1983). *Outrageous acts and everyday rebellions.* New York: Holt, Rinehart and Winston.

Waber, D. P. (1977). Sex differences in mental abilities, hemispheric lateralization, and rate of physical growth at adolescence. *Developmental Psychology, 13,* 29–38.

Wilkie, F. L., & Eisdorfer, C. (1977). Sex, verbal ability, and pacing differences in serial learning. *Journal of Gerontology, 32,* 63–67.

Wine, J. D.; Moses, B.; & Smye, M. D.(1980). Female superiority in sex-difference competence comparisons: A review of the literature. In C. Stark-Adamec (Ed.), *Sex roles: Origins, influences, and implications for women* (pp. 148–163). Montreal: Eden Press Women's Publications.

CHAPTER
ELEVEN

# SHOULD WOMEN'S RELATIONAL ABILITIES BE CALLED "DEPENDENCY"?

As researchers through the years have studied sex differences in various kinds of behavior and personality traits, they have usually given respectful labels to the ones found to be more common among males but demeaning labels to those found to be more common among females (Wine, Moses, & Smye, 1980). For instance, it is widely claimed that males are more "assertive"—a desirable, high-status term, and that females are more "dependent"—an undesirable, low-status term. In general, those labels given to males' behavior have also tended to be associated with emotional maturity (like assertiveness) and those given to females' behavior, with immaturity (like dependency). Wine and her colleagues (1980) have said that skills and behavior reported as more frequently found in males tend to be described as essential or basic, such as "rational thinking," whereas those reported as more frequently found in females are described as nonessential or lower level, such as "caretaking behavior." Even some feminist researchers have described some behavior typically found in girls and women as "over concern" with social factors rather than "concern" or "healthy concern" (Wine et al., 1980, pp. 151–152).

One result of this widespread pattern has been that many girls and women feel embarrassed and ashamed about their behavior, worrying continually that they are being "too" dependent, "too" emotional, "too" sensitive, and so on. A related result has been that, because typically male behavior has been treated with such respect, many boys and men have never thought to question whether anything in their behavior needs improvement.

In this chapter, we shall first examine the question, "Does the research justify labeling females as dependent and overly emotional?" and the related question, "Does the research justify labeling males as assertive?" Then we shall consider some recent writing which offers powerful new ways to interpret research related to this question.

## ❖ DEPENDENCY AND EMOTIONS

Even if a research study is carefully designed and the data are properly collected, the researcher has enormous power in interpreting and labeling the findings. If research truly demonstrated that men can take care of themselves but women cannot, and that men can calmly and firmly state their opinions and feelings but women cannot, then we might feel justified in calling women dependent and men assertive. But that is *not* what the research has shown. Most studies that have been used to "prove" that women are the more dependent and less assertive sex are studies of behavior that do not actually seem to be about dependency and assertiveness. Wine and her associates (1980) reviewed a great deal of sex-difference research that was published in the late 1960s and 1970s which has been used to "prove" that females are more dependent than males. They found that research *actually* showed that females tend more than males to:

> look at other people (Argyle & Cook, 1976; Exline, 1972)

> listen, pay attention, and respond to the speaker more, interrupt less, and time their responses well so that the other person doesn't change or drop the subject (Argyle, Lalljee, & Cook, 1968; Markel, Long, & Saine, 1976; Weitz, 1976; Zimmerman & West, 1975)

> do more nonaggressive touching (Whiting & Edwards, 1973)

> stand and sit closer to same-sex people (Baxter, 1970; Heshka & Nelson, 1972; Mehrabian & Diamond, 1971)

> be accurate senders and interpreters of emotion-related messages (Rosenthal, Archer, DiMatteo, Koivumaki, & Rogers, 1974; Rosenthal, Hall, DiMatteo, Rogers, & Archer, 1977; Zuckerman, Lipets, Koivumaki, & Rosenthal, 1975)

> talk more about their friends and themselves (Cozby, 1973; Hottes & Kahn, 1974)

> change their behavior depending upon the other person's behavior and how well they know them (Heshka & Nelson, 1972; Weitz, 1976; Willis, 1966)

> smile more (Cline & Spender, 1987; Mackey, 1976)

> have more positive, friendly, and encouraging interactions with strangers (Stark-Adamec & Pihl, 1978)

Using studies like these, many researchers concluded that females are emotionally dependent (see Rachel Josefowitz Siegel's 1988 paper for a discussion of this labeling).

After reading the above descriptions of the kinds of behavior that were studied, you might not think the term "dependency" is appropriate for them. However, lecturers and writers often begin by claiming that females are dependent and then offer as "proof" the information that, for instance, females look at other people more than do males; then the audience unquestioningly assumes that looking at people is indeed a sign of emotional neediness or dependency. But recently, a number of theorists have offered a whole new way of thinking about this kind of research. In a paper called "Women's 'dependency' in a male-centered value system" (1988), social worker Rachel Josefowitz Siegel proposes that we assign an apt label to the behavior that has been mislabeled *dependency,* and for that purpose she suggests the term *interdependence.* This term, she points out, does not have negative connotations and does have appropriately positive, mature ones. For women and for men who have felt ashamed about displaying characteristics such as concern about and responsiveness to other people, this relabeling can transform their views of themselves, significantly enhancing their self-esteem. Similarly, psychologist Janet Surrey (1985) has proposed the terms *relational abilities* and *self-in-relation* to replace such labels as *dependency and immaturity, respectively,* for the kinds of behavior listed earlier. Surrey and several of her colleagues have written about many aspects of personality and interpersonal relationships from this new perspective (many of these papers are collected in the book *Women's growth in connection,* edited by Judith Jordan, Alexandra Kaplan, Jean Baker Miller, Irene Stiver, and Janet Surrey, 1991). For instance, Judith Jordan has drawn attention to the nature and importance of empathy in relationships.

Psychologist Nikki Gerrard (1987, 1988) has described the way that Surrey's term, *relational abilities,* can help us to think differently, and often more productively, about human relationships. Until recently, most of the theorists about human development have named independence and autonomy as the major aims (Miller, 1984). Although it is true that independence and autonomy *are* important goals for development, so, too, are the goals of increasing and expanding the variety of abilities that help us form relationships, express and understand our own feelings and the feelings of others, and so on (Miller, 1984). But because of the traditional emphasis on independence, psychotherapists and counselors to whom people have turned when feeling depressed or upset have often jumped to the conclusion that those feelings result from the people being "overly dependent." Gerrard, as a trained therapist herself, writes that she had been heavily influenced by the focus on independence. So, when her daughter, Sarah, was acting upset and wanting her to play with her one Sunday, Gerrard jumped to the conclusion that she had failed to teach Sarah to play independently. Worried that playing with Sarah would just reinforce that lack of independence, she tried to get Sarah to play by herself, but those efforts failed miserably. Then, Gerrard recalled Surrey's paper about relational abilities and asked herself whether Sarah's upset might have been due to feeling lonesome and distant. So, she took Sarah in her arms and expressed her love for her. Almost immediately, Sarah jumped up and happily ran off to play by herself. When mother and daughter reconnected emotionally, the daughter then felt happier and more secure and thus more relaxed about playing independently. Had Gerrard focused *only* on independence, rather than on the interplay between connectedness and independence within the relationship, the problem would not have been solved.

This story illustrates how destructive the overemphasis on independence as a measure of psychological health has been. It has been assumed that females are more dependent—and therefore deficient—than males, rather than taking the attitude that females have learned to care—admirably—about feelings and connections with other people. This has been damaging to people of both sexes in different ways. Girls and women have been taught, on the one hand, that they are *supposed to* develop relational abilities and to care about others, but then those very abilities and concerns have been labeled as signs of their immaturity or even of their mental illness. Boys and men have been taught to suppress their "feminine" feelings of concern about human connections, and few have been encouraged to develop their skills in interacting with others, recognizing and expressing feelings, and so on. In fact, some males have even been discouraged from developing those skills.

Women and men have often reported feeling enormously relieved when they have read Siegel's and the Wellesley group's work, because they discover that some of their feelings and behavior are not dependent and immature, as they have thought. For instance, they say, "I had been ashamed of myself for longing to have a close, loving relationship with one person. I thought that meant that I was overly dependent. Then I read Siegel's article and realized that it just means that I have some normal, common, human needs for an emotional connection and interaction with other people!"

## ❖ ARE FEMALES MORALLY INFERIOR TO MALES?

Females' concern with feelings and relationships has been used to argue that they are less developed than men in moral reasoning. One of the most famous modern theorists to conduct research about development of moral reasoning was Lawrence Kohlberg, who said his work demonstrated females' underdevelopment in that area. Kohlberg (1964, 1966, 1973, 1976; Kohlberg & Kramer, 1969) studied moral development by presenting people with a series of stories about moral dilemmas and asking them to tell what they thought the main character in each one should do and, most importantly, *why* they thought the person should act that way; for instance, in one story a man's wife had a fatal illness, and the couple could not afford the high cost of the drug that could help her. The druggist refused the husband's request to sell the drug more cheaply or let him pay later, so the husband broke into the store to steal the drug. Respondents were asked to say whether or not they thought the husband should have stolen the drug and *why* they thought that (e.g., because saving a human life is the most important thing, because you should never break a law, etc.; Kohlberg, 1976).

Based on his research with people at various ages, Kohlberg said he had discovered a series of stages of moral development through which everyone passes as they grow; for instance, at one of the early stages, people make decisions about moral issues in certain ways in order to avoid being punished, whereas at higher stages they make moral decisions based on fundamental principles, such as the value of human life. Kohlberg reported further that not everyone reaches the highest stages and that, in general, females' moral reasoning tends to stop at lower stages than that of males. These claims were and still are widely believed to be true. What Kohlberg (1976; Kohlberg & Kramer, 1969) said specifically about females was that their moral development tended to stop at the third of his six stages. At the third stage, moral decisions are based on concerns about interpersonal relationships and helping others. Thus, "the very traits that traditionally have defined the 'goodness' of women, their care for and sensitivity to the needs of others, are those that mark them as deficient in moral development" (Gilligan, 1982, p. 18).

Some years after Kohlberg's influential work was published, Carol Gilligan wrote an extremely important book called *In a Different Voice* (1982), in which she raised questions about Kohlberg's work and also reported research of her own. She had worked with Kohlberg and knew that the research he had used to identify the stages of moral development had been done with 84 males whose race was unspecified (it is likely, however, that most or all were white). She pointed out that when you "discover" stages by studying only one group, it is not surprising if a group that has been socialized very differently does not show that same pattern. And if the latter group doesn't show the same pattern, that should not be assumed to prove that that group is defective or immature. What Kohlberg *may* have uncovered (though his group was very small to form the basis of a theory of such importance) was not a universal set of stages but rather the stages through which North American (probably white) males tend to go.

Gilligan also expressed concern that Kohlberg's stories were often far removed from the real experiences the participants might have had. So she conducted a study of her own, this time using only female participants and a very real moral dilemma they were facing at that time: whether or not to have an abortion. Whereas Kohlberg's "highly moral" men based their moral decisions on such abstract principles as "justice," Gilligan found that the women she studied tried to find ways to achieve the greatest good for the greatest number of people. If Gilligan had used Kohlberg's stages to classify the women in her study, they would have been considered relatively poorly developed or deficient in terms of their moral reasoning.

As with many sex-difference issues, scholars debate whether the differences between Kohlberg's males and Gilligan's females are innate or learned. But perhaps Gilligan's most important accomplishment has been her presentation of a caring, people-oriented approach to morality (with all the "messiness" that comes when we don't simply resort to abstract principles), as deserving of respect rather than as low-level, irrational, and dependent.

One interesting consequence of the kinds of work done by Siegel, Surrey, Jordan, Miller, Kaplan, Stiver, and Gilligan has been the dignifying of whole new realms of psychology as worthy of attention and study. Traditionally, some kinds of psychological research have been considered higher status and worthier of study than others. Usually, those researchers working on such topics as achievement, competition, and independence or autonomy (which are usually associated with males) have been more respected than those working on nurturance, empathy, or what has been called "dependency" (which are usually associated with females).

Before we leave this topic, we should point out that, if Kohlberg's work was flawed because he studied only males and used only hypothetical situations, Gilligan studied only females who were facing an immediate and intensely personal dilemma (for an evaluation of Gilligan's work, see Colby & Damon, 1983). Thus, it might be useful, if one wanted to explore sex differences in morality, to study a wide variety and large number of people of both sexes as they react to a wide variety of actual and theoretical dilemmas.

## ❖ ASSERTIVENESS

If women *were* truly more dependent than men, it would not be particularly surprising if they were also less assertive. And indeed, the mistaken belief in females' dependency has helped pave the way for the belief that females are unassertive. Here, too, research has been used as "evidence" of females' lack of assertiveness. But let us look at what the research actually shows.

First of all, very few studies of real assertiveness have been conducted, and "there is surprisingly little empirical evidence in the literature which directly supports the assumption that females are less skilled than males in interpersonal interactions calling for assertiveness" (Smye, Wine, & Moses, 1980, p. 165). Some research does show that females *describe themselves* as less assertive than the way males describe themselves (Galassi, DeLeo, Galassi, & Bastien, 1974; Rathus, 1973), but the way people describe themselves is often very different from the way they really act. This is especially true when social expectations come into play. Since males are *expected* to be assertive and females to be less so, the differences in the ways they describe their assertiveness might be entirely a consequence of what they think they should say.

Furthermore, many studies of other kinds of behavior have been mistakenly classified as studies of assertiveness, usually resulting in the casting of males in a favorable light; for instance, many of the studies cited in the list at the beginning of this chapter—such as who interrupts more, who responds less to other people's comments, and so on—have been used to shore up claims that males are more assertive. In fact, however, those are not really studies of assertiveness. As Smye and her colleagues point out (1980), when assertiveness has supposedly been studied, *aggressiveness* has usually been included as a crucial component, and men are socialized to behave more aggressively than women.

Let us look at what happened when researchers studied actual assertiveness by using such measures as eye contact, self-expression, and assertion of an independent stance—kinds of behavior that fit definitions of assertiveness without including aggressiveness or rudeness. Smye et al. (1980) had people of both sexes react to a wide variety of social situations, ranging from receiving compliments to requests for help to attacks on their (the respondents') appearance or on themselves as people (Smye et al., 1980). The females in that study showed more appropriately assertive behavior, such as eye contact, self-expression, and asserting an independent stance, than did the males.

## ❖ A REVEALING PAIR OF STUDIES

The importance of investigating and thinking carefully before declaring that one has discovered a sex difference in behavior is illustrated dramatically by a pair of studies that were done on the same group of children. In 1969, Goldberg and Lewis claimed that their research showed girls to be dependent and boys to be independent. They had studied 16 children of each sex who were 6 months old and another 16 of each sex who were 13 months old. Each mother had held her child on her lap in a room filled with toys and then placed the child on the floor. After 15 minutes had passed, a mesh barrier in a wooden frame with a latch was placed in the middle of the room, with the mother on one side and the child on the other. Each mother-child pair was observed for a total of 30 minutes.

According to Goldberg and Lewis, during the entire session more girls returned immediately to their mothers, returned sooner, returned more often both physically and visually (by looking at them) and looked longer, vocalized more to their mothers, and stayed closer to their mothers. After the barrier had been put in place, the girls cried and motioned for help more, and the boys made more active attempts to get around the barrier. Based on these results, Goldberg and Lewis (1969) concluded that the girls were more dependent and showed less exploratory behavior and that the boys were independent and showed more exploratory behavior.

For 10 years after the Goldberg and Lewis study was published, their conclusions were quoted widely as evidence of females' greater emotional dependency and males' greater independence and "problem-solving ability." This sex difference was thought to show how, even in the first year of life, females' greater emotionality and helplessness and males' greater practicality or rationality were evident. And many people took the step from there to the conclusion that if the difference appears so early, it must be innate, instinctual, and, therefore, inevitable. Some even claimed it would be wrong to try to change such behavior *because* it was supposedly innate and natural.

Then, in 1979, Feiring and Lewis reported what had happened when the same children from the Goldberg and Lewis study were observed in the same situation at 25 months of age. They found that at that age, the girls spent more time manipulating the latch and vocalizing to their mothers, and the boys spent more time fretting and looking at their mothers. Seven of the girls but only two of the boys undid the latch and were able to get out from behind the barrier. According to Feiring and Lewis, "in terms of problem solving" when the barrier was present girls spent the most time vocalizing, while boys spent the most time crying. Girls used two-word utterances and the word "out" and referred to the barrier more than boys.

"To summarize," write Feiring and Lewis, "at 2 years of age . . . girls spent more time in problem-solving behavior. . . , while boys showed more emotional upset" (p. 851). This kind of emotional upset would probably have been called "dependency" by Goldberg and Lewis. Furthermore, note Feiring and Lewis, "Although both boys and girls do [as they get older] increase the amount of time spent manipulating the latch, boys did not show a significant increase from 1 to 2 years, while girls did" (p. 851). Feiring and Lewis conclude: "At 2 years of age, girls appeared to use more mature instrumental acts for coping with this frustrating situation" (p. 851).

This pair of studies shows how risky it is to draw conclusions about sex differences in behavior by studying children at just one point in their lives and then trying to determine what behavior is innate. Especially if we believe there is definitely a particular sex difference in adults, such as "Women are more dependent," it is tempting simply to assume that a study such as the one by Goldberg and Lewis reveals innate differences. Another, related mistake is to assume that the kind of pattern the children showed in the first year of life (which might have been interpreted as females being more dependent and males being better at problem-solving) will persist, unchanged, into adulthood. And, as seen throughout this chapter, no matter whom we study or when we study them, we must take the greatest care in choosing labels for their behavior.

Another important lesson is that, in any given culture, the kinds of behavior least respected and valued are probably in danger of being labeled by the so-called experts as signs of immaturity, as inappropriate conduct, or as otherwise undesirable. In a society in which white, middle-class males tend to be treated with greater respect than members of other groups, it is likely that behavior associated with them will be treated as evidence of maturity and solid emotional adjustment. Thus, the work on dependency, relational abilities, and labeling of behavior becomes especially crucial in helping us to sort out what is and is not healthy, what does and does not make our lives happier.

# References

Argyle, M., & Cook, M. (1976). *Gaze and mutual gaze.* Cambridge: Cambridge University Press.

Argyle, M.; Lalljee, M.; & Cook, M. (1968). The effects of visibility on interaction in a dyad. *Human Relations, 21,* 3–17.

Baxter, C. (1970). Interpersonal spacing in natural settings. *Sociometry, 33,* 444–456.

Cline, S., & Spender, D. (1987). *Reflecting men at twice their natural size.* London: Andre Deutsch.

Colby, A., & Damon, W. (1983). Listening to a different voice: A review of Gilligan's *In a different voice. Merrill-Palmer Quarterly, 29,* 473–481.

Cozby, P. G. (1973). Self disclosure: A literature review. *Psychological Bulletin, 79,* 73–91.

Exline, R. V. (1972). Visual interaction: The glances of power and preference. In J. Cole (Ed.), *Nebraska symposium on motivation* (pp. 65–92). Lincoln, NE: Nebraska University Press.

Feiring, C., & Lewis, M. (1979). Sex and age differences in young children's reactions to frustration: A further look at the Goldberg and Lewis subjects. *Child Development, 50,* 848–853.

Galassi, J. P.; DeLeo, J. S.; Galassi, M. D.; & Bastien, S. (1974). The College Self-Expression Scale: A measure of assertiveness. *Behavior Therapy, 5,* 165–171.

Gerrard, N. (1987, May). *A critical analysis of guilt in relation to mothers and daughters.* Paper presented at the Feminist Therapists' Association Annual Meeting, Toronto.

Gerrard, N. (1988). Undoing crazymaking: Feminist therapy—a stitch in time saves nine. *Popular Feminism Lecture Series Paper No. 7.* Centre for Women's Studies in Education, Ontario Institute for Studies in Education, Toronto.

Gilligan, C. (1982). *In a different voice.* Cambridge, MA: Harvard University Press.

Goldberg, S., & Lewis, M. (1969). Play behavior in the year-old infant: Early sex differences. *Child Development, 40,* 21–31.

Heshka, S., & Nelson, Y. (1972). Interpersonal speaking distance as a function of age, sex and relationship. *Sociometry, 35,* 491–498.

Hottes, J. J., & Kahn, A. (1974). Sex differences in a mixed-motive confflict situation. *Journal of Personality, 42,* 260–275.

Jordan, J.; Kaplan, A.; Miller, J. B.; Stiver, I.; & Surrey, J. (1991). *Women's growth in connection.* New York: Guilford.

Kohlberg, L. (1981). *The philosophy of moral development.* San Francisco: Harper & Row.

Kohlberg, L. (1976). Moral stages and moralization: The cognitive-developmental approach. In T. Lickona (Ed.), *Moral development and behavior: Theory, research, and social issues.* New York: Holt, Rinehart and Winston.

Kohlberg, L. (1973). Continuities and discontinuities in childhood and adult moral development revisited. In *Collected papers on moral development and moral education.* Moral Education Research Foundation, Harvard University.

Kohlberg, L. (1966). A cognitive-developmental analysis of children's sex-role concepts and attitudes. In E. Maccoby (Ed.), *The development of sex differences* (pp. 82–172). Stanford, CA: Stanford University Press.

Kohlberg, L. (1964). Development of moral character and moral ideology. In M. L. Hoffman & L.W. Hoffman (Eds.), *Review of child development research* (pp. 383–432). New York: Russell Sage Foundation.

Kohlberg, L., & Kramer, R. (1969). Continuities and discontinuities in child and adult moral development. *Human Development, 12,* 93–120.

Mackey, W. C. (1976). Parameters of the smile as a social signal. *Journal of Genetic Psychology, 129,* 125–130.

Markel, N. N.; Long, J. F.; & Saine, I. J. (1976). Sex effects in conversational interactions: Another look at male dominance. *Human Communication Research, 2,* 356–364.

Mehrabian, A., & Diamond, S. G. (1971). Effects of furniture arrangements, props, and personality on social interaction. *Journal of Personality and Social Psychology, 20,* 18–30.

Miller, J. B. (1984). *The development of women's sense of self.* Work in Progress, No. 12. Wellesley College, Wellesley, MA.

Rathus, S. A. (1973). A 30-item schedule for assessing assertive behavior. *Behavior Therapy, 4,* 398–406.

Rosenthal, R.; Archer, D.; DiMatteo, M. R.; Koivumaki, J. H.; & Rogers, P. L. (1974, September). Body talk and tone of voice: The language without words. *Psychology Today,* pp. 64–68.

Rosenthal, R.; Hall, J. A.; DiMatteo, R.; Rogers, P. L.; & Archer, D. (1977). *Sensitivity to non-verbal communication: The PONS test.* Unpublished monograph, Harvard University.

Siegel, R. J. (1988). Women's "dependency" in a male-centered value system: Gender-based values regarding dependency and independence. *Women and Therapy, 7,* 113–123.

Smye, M. D.; Wine, J. D.; & Moses, B. (1980). Sex differences in assertiveness: Implications for research and treatment. In Cannie Stark-Adamec (Ed.), *Sex roles: Origins, influences, and implications for women* (pp. 164–175). Montreal: Eden Press Women's Publications.

Stark-Adamec, C., & Pihl, R. O. (1978). Sex differences in response to marijuana in a social setting. *Psychology of Women Quarterly, 2(4),* 334–353.

Surrey, J. (1985). *The "self-in-relation": A theory of women's development.* Work in Progress, No. 13, Stone Center, Wellesley, MA.

Weitz, S. (1976). Sex differences in nonverbal communication. *Sex Roles, 2,* 175–184.

Whiting, B., & Edwards, C. (1973). A cross-cultural analysis of sex differences in the behavior of children aged 3 through 11. *Journal of Psychology, 91,* 171–188.

Willis, F. N., Jr. (1966). Initial speaking distance as a function of the speakers' relationship. *Psychonomic Science, 5,* 221–222.

Wine, J. D.; Moses, B.; & Smye, M. D. (1980). Female superiority in sex difference competence comparisons: A review of the literature. In C. Stark-Adamec (Ed.), *Sex roles: Origins, influences, and implications for women* (pp. 148–163). Montreal: Eden Press Women's Publications.

Zimmerman, D. H., & West, C. (1975). Sex roles, interruptions, and silence in conversation. In B. Thorne & N. Henley (Eds.), *Language and sex: Difference and dominance.* Rowley, MA: Newbury House.

Zuckerman, N.; Lipets, M. S.; Koivumaki, J. H.; & Rosenthal, R. (1975). Encoding and decoding nonverbal cues of emotion. *Journal of Personality and Social Psychology, 32,* 1068–1076.

# CHAPTER
# TWELVE

# BREAKING THE CYCLE OF BIAS: BECOMING AN INFORMED JUDGE OF RESEARCH

Our aim in writing this book has been *not* to convince you of the truth of any particular fact about males or about females but rather to help you become an informed thinker who can skillfully assess the claims you hear or read about sex or gender. This is important because every day we are exposed to a great many sex-role stereotypes. Sometimes they are explicitly stated ("Boys are more aggressive than girls," "Real men don't like romantic poetry," "A good woman doesn't think about her own needs"), and sometimes they are implicit (as when the head of an engineering faculty plans a male-focused orientation week for new students). To be able to free yourself from the narrow view of life that such stereotypes create, it is crucial to become aware of these stereotypes, of the research on which they are based, and of some common problems in that research.

As you have gathered by now, it is extremely difficult to design and carry out high-quality research on sex and gender, and yet most people in their daily lives behave as though most sex-role stereotypes have been proven to be unquestionably true. This has often fed the continuing, sex-stereotypic restrictions on the behavior of both sexes ("You can't do that! Boys/Girls don't do such things. It's unnatural") and especially the treatment of girls and women as inferior. In the preceding chapters, you have read in detail about various kinds of research problems. As you went through the chapters on specific areas of sex-difference research, you probably noticed that some of the research errors were mentioned in relation to more than one area. Keep in mind that every research problem mentioned in this book was chosen because it is commonly found to mar widely believed research in a number of areas related to sex and gender. In fact, nearly every one of the following research problems appears in some form or other in almost every one of the topic chapters (Chapter 4 through Chapter 11):

Definitional problems

Basing research questions on sexist or otherwise biased assumptions or theories

Using inappropriate, inadequate, or invalid tests and other methods of measurement (including content that is much more familiar or unthreatening to one sex than to the other)

Investigating only certain kinds of people but claiming to have found a sex difference, as though it applies to all people

Inaccurately or irresponsibly reporting and/or interpreting the data

Inappropriately using (some) animals' behavior to "explain" humans' behavior

"Box score" errors (ignoring some studies when summarizing the research on a particular topic)

Exaggerating the size and/or stability of sex differences

Ignoring or downplaying of overlap in females' and males' performance or behavior (and of no-difference results)

Assuming too hastily that a sex difference is innate

Creating theories not supported by or inadequately supported by the available research data (including theories based on only some of the data)

As you have read, when you encounter any claim about any group or any difference between groups, you can consider:

1. What might be the researchers' motives for doing this research? Whether the speaker is a researcher or an acquaintance at a cocktail party making some claim about sex differences, ask yourself why that speaker has such an intense need to believe in, or search for, sex differences. Keep in mind that an equally intense focus on racial differences has long been recognized as a form of racism, whereas the deeply sexist bias involved in looking frenetically for sex differences is not widely acknowledged.

2. Are certain kinds of bias reflected in the way the *research question* was asked?

3. Are there *methodological problems* with the way the research was designed and carried out?

4. Did the researchers *interpret* their data in reasonable or in biased ways?

5. Even if the researchers' interpretation of their data seems plausible, what *alternative explanations* or *rival hypotheses* (Huck & Sandler, 1979) might also account for these data?

Above all, we hope that you have a clear understanding of the fact that scientists are not objective and certainly not infallible. We hope that you have seen that political philosophies, personal feelings, and a host of other factors can shape the research questions that are asked, the way research is done, and the ways the results are interpreted and then applied in educational, workplace, social, and political situations. With this understanding and the tools to ask important questions about research, rather than having to accept what you are told, you can help to break the cycle of bias.

# Reference

Huck, S. W., & Sandler, H. M. (1979). *Rival hypotheses: Alternative interpretations of data-based conclusions.* New York: Harper & Row.

# SUGGESTIONS FOR FURTHER READING AND PRACTICE

To practice your skills in critical thinking about research on sex and gender, you can pick up popular magazines such as *Discover* and *Psychology Today*, as well as the sections about psychology or human behavior in *U.S. News & World Report, Time,* or *Newsweek.* All of those publications frequently have articles about recent research or theory about sex and gender. So, too, do daily newspapers and—sometimes—the magazines that come with newspapers. Try reading any relevant articles and asking the kinds of questions that are illustrated throughout this book.

If you can locate a copy of a wonderful but, unfortunately, out-of-print book called *Rival Hypotheses: Alternative Interpretations of Data-based Conclusions* (by Schuyler W. Huck and Howard M. Sandler; published in New York by Harper & Row, 1979), you can have a great time. The book is filled with one-page reports of psychological research on a variety of subjects. The reader is asked to read one report at a time, find every research error that you think is illustrated by that report, and then try to come up with alternative ways to interpet the data presented in the report. In the back of the book, there is an answer guide, in which Huck and Sandler tell you what research errors and alternative interpretations they themselves found for each report.

And here is a list of other references about research methods and statistics that you may wish to consult:

Agnew, N. McK., & Pyke, S. W. (1982). *The science game: An introduction to research in the behavioral sciences.* Englewood Cliffs, NJ: Prentice-Hall.

Campbell, D. T., & Stanley, J. C. (1966). *Experimental and quasi-experimental designs for research.* Chicago: Rand-McNally.

Eichler, M. (1988). *Nonsexist research methods: A practical guide.* Boston: Allen & Unwin.

Eichler, M. (1980). *The double standard: A feminist critique of feminist social science.* London: Croom Helm.

Eichler, M., & Lapointe, J. (1985). *On the treatment of the sexes in research/Le traitement objectif des sexes dans la recherche.* Ottawa: Social Sciences and Humanities Research Council of Canada/Conseil de recherches en sciences humaines du Canada.

Freedman, D.; Pisani, R.; & Purves, R. (1978). *Statistics.* New York: Norton.

Guilford, J. P. (1965). *Fundamental statistics in psychology and education.* New York: McGraw-Hill.

Huck, S. W.; Cormier, W. H.; & Bounds, W. G., Jr. (1974). *Reading statistics and research.* New York: Harper & Row.

Huff, D. (1954). *How to lie with statistics.* New York: Norton.

Mahoney, M. J. (1976). *Scientist as subject: The psychological imperative.* Cambridge, MA: Ballinger.

McHugh, M. C.; Koeske, R. D.; & Frieze, I. H. (1986). Issues to consider in conducting nonsexist research: A guide for researchers. *American Psychologist, 41,* 879–890.

Roscoe, J. T. (1975). *Fundamental research statistics for the behavioral sciences.* New York: Holt, Rinehart and Winston.

Rosenthal, R. (1963). On the social psychology of the psychological experiment: The experimenter's hypothesis as an unintended determinant of experimental results. *American Scientist, 51,* 268–283.

Webb, F. J.; Campbell, D. T.; Schwartz, R. D.; & Sechrest, L. (1966). *Unobtrusive measures: Non-reactive research in the social sciences.* Chicago: Rand McNally.

Winer, B. J. (1962). *Statistical principles in experimental design.* New York: McGraw-Hill.

Other superb books and articles we encourage you to inspect are:

Bleier, R. (1984). *Science and gender.* New York: Pergamon Press.

Bleier, R. (Ed.). (1986). *Feminist approaches to science.* New York: Pergamon Press.

Fausto-Sterling, A . (1992). *Myths of gender: Biological theories about women and men.* Second Edition. New York: Basic Books.

Greenglass, E. (1982). *A world of difference: Gender roles in perspective.* Toronto: Wiley.

Hare-Mustin, R. T., & Maracek, J. (1988). The meaning of difference: Gender theory, postmodernism, and psychology. *American Psychologist, 43,* 455–464.

Hubbard, R. (1990). *The politics of women's biology.* New Brunswick, NJ: Rutgers University Press.

Keller, E. F. (1985). *Reflections on gender and science.* New Haven, CT: Yale University Press.

Tavris, C. (1992). *The mismeasure of woman.* New York: Simon & Schuster.

Walsh, M. R. (Ed.). (1987). *The psychology of women: Ongoing debates.* New Haven, CT: Yale University Press.c

You might also wish to hone your skills by listening to discussions in different classes and in social situations with family or friends. When anyone makes a claim about sex differences—or racial, age, sexual orientation, social class, or physical or mental ability differences—stop and think about the kinds of questions and research problems we have discussed in the previous chapters. You will probably discover that you find it harder than before to take other people's unsupported claims as the truth—and that makes for a healthier society.

# NAME
# INDEX

# SUBJECT INDEX

Accuracy of measuring instrument, 24–25
Adolescence, sex differences after, 32, 33
Ageism, 78
Aggressiveness
 males', 81, 104–105
  beliefs about innateness of, 60–63
  excusing, 65–66, 78
  testosterone and, 62–63
  theories of, 60–63
  against women and children, 49–50, 64, 65–66, 75
 sex-difference research about, 63–66
  boundary conditions in, 63–64
  definitional problems, 59–60
  social and political consequences of assumptions of, 64–65
 socialization and, 64
Alternative explanations, consideration of, 111
Assertiveness
 social expectations and, 104–105
 label of, 99, 100
 research about, 104–105
Assumptions, incorrect, 110. See also Experimenter bias
 about ability to predict about individuals on basis of average scores, 3
 about aggressive behavior of men, 60–66

in Benbow and Stanley research, 39
dangerous, in sex-difference research, 2–4
failing to question, 17
about intellectual inferiority of women, 12–15
maintenance of status quo and, 12–13
about males' superiority in mathematics, 39–45
about masochism and women, 52–53
about menopause, 77–78
that sex differences are biologically based, 3–4

Bad mother myths, 73
Battered women, 49–50
 treatment of, by therapists, 50
Beliefs, of researchers. See Assumptions, incorrect; Experimenter bias
Bias. See Experimenter bias
Blood sampling, and skewing of results, 82
Boundary condition, 63–64
Brain functioning, 6
 and brain size, claims about, 13–14, 17
 problems with studies of, 33

Racism, 16, 32, 78
Rape, 65
Reading skills, interpretation of sex differences in, 15
Relational abilities, sex-difference reseach about, 100–106
Religion, 12
Research, about sex-differences. *See* Sex-difference research
Research problems. *See* Methodological errors
Research questions
  biases in, 110
  experimenter bias in choice of, 85–86, 110
Retrospective reports, unreliability of, 82

Samples
  inadequate, 82
  uniform, problem of obtaining, 40–41
Sampling error, 25–26
  in Benbow and Stanley study, 42–43
Science, in the nineteenth century, 12–15
Scientific method, 6, 12, 19
  defined, 19
  using, to study sex and gender, 6, 19–28
Self-reported observations, 25, 82
Sex, defined, 4
Sex-difference research. *See also* Methodological errors
  about aggression, 7, 63–66
  assumptions made in. *See* Assumptions, incorrect; Experimenter bias
  awareness of limitations of, 20, 28
  becoming informed judge of, 109–111
  bias in, 1–2, 7–8, 12–17
  choice of question in, 20, 85–86
  common research problems in, 110
  considerations in evaluating, 110–111
  critical thinking about, goals for, 5–6
  dangerous assumptions in, 2–4

definitional problems in. *See* Definitional problems
design problems, 21–24
errors in interpretation of results, 26–27
historical perspective on, 6, 11–17
labeling of male/female behavior in, 99–102, 106
about mathematical abilities, 6–7, 37–45
methods used in, 21–24
perspective needed for study of, 7–9
political nature of, 85–86
problematic patterns in, 16–17
problems in carrying out, 24–26
results of, 100
about spatial abilities, 7, 29–34
status of, 104
suggested readings, 113–114
about verbal abilities, 7
Sex differences
  characteristics of, 32–33
  as female deficiencies, 77–78
Sexism, 72, 78
  racism in combination with, 32
Sex-role stereotypes, 38, 49–50, 56, 59, 77, 85, 89–90, 95–96, 99–100, 104, 109
Skewed results
  blood sampling and, 82
  causes of, 22–26
Small difference results
  in aggression studies, 63
  exaggerating, 110
  in mathematical abilities research, 37
  in spatial abilities research, 32
  in verbal abilities research, 94
Social Darwinism, 15–16
Society, and gender, 4–5
Spatial abilities
  brain lateralization theories of, 33
  flaws in theories about, 33–34
  genetic theory of, 33
  sex-difference research about, 7, 29–34, 91, 94
    definitional problems, 29–31
    extent of sex differences in, 32–33
    flawed theories and, 33–34
    measuring instruments in, 34
    no-difference results in, 32–33